'People want to create their own homes to suit their own lives'

TERENCE CONRAN

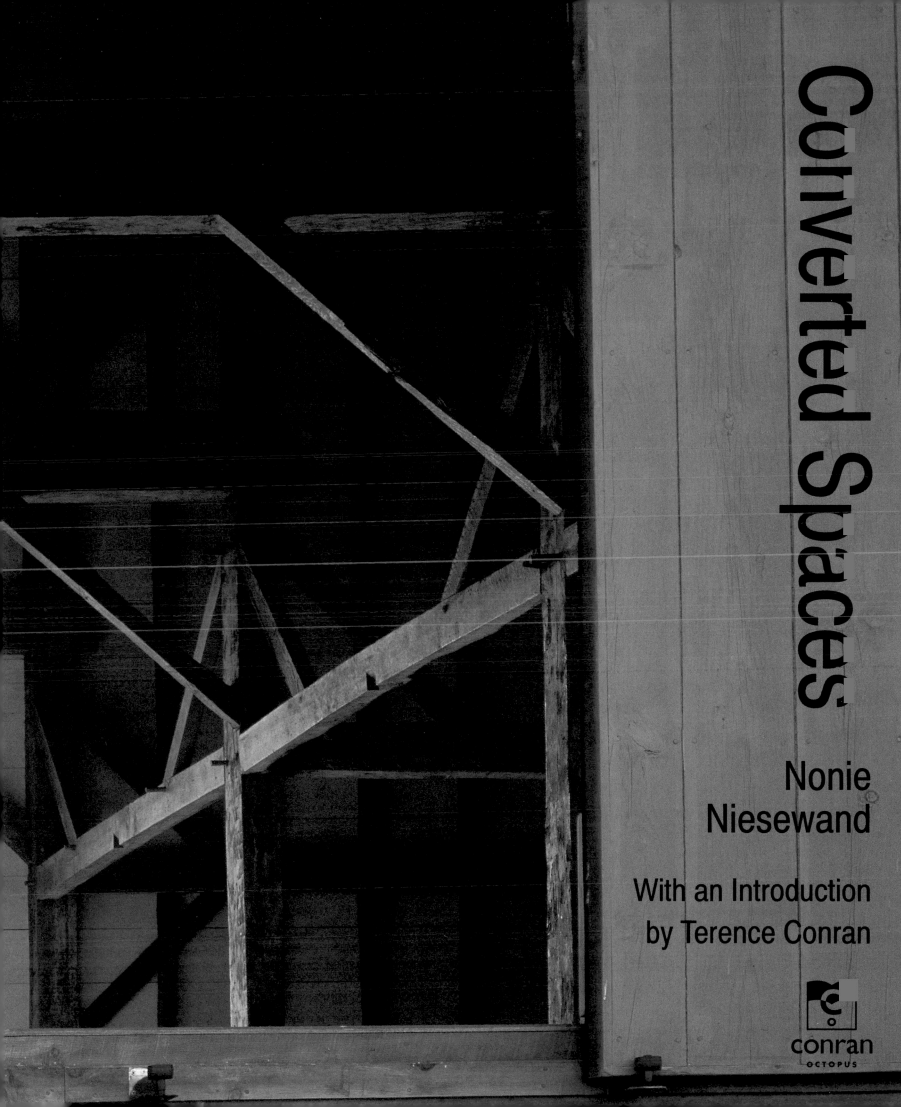

Converted Spaces

Nonie
Niesewand

With an Introduction
by Terence Conran

conran
OCTOPUS

First published in 1998 by
Conran Octopus Limited
37 Shelton Street
London WC2H 9HN

Commissioning Editor: Denny Hemming
Managing Editor: Catriona Woodburn
Editorial: Paula Hardy, Phyllis Richardson,
    Kate Quarry
Design: Paul Welti
Gatefold plans: Tony Seddon
Picture Research: Jess Walton, Jo Walton
Production: Mano Mylvaganam, Jill Beed

British Library Cataloguing-in-Publication Data
A catalogue record for this book is available from
the British Library
ISBN 1 85029 951 X

Printed in China

Contents

Introduction

Terence Conran

Space is perhaps the greatest luxury of the modern age. How we use it, and particularly how we live in it, requires a complex balancing act between practical limitations, individual requirements and personal preferences. In the post-industrial cities of North America, Europe and Australia, abandoned factories and warehouses have – like empty schools and churches, banks and garage showrooms – provided large open spaces in which people have chosen to make their homes.

One of the greatest appeals of the 'loft living' phenomenon is that it frees people to create a domestic environment that expresses their style of life. No longer bound by the constraints of the traditional house, people often find themselves with just four walls, a floor and a ceiling as their starting point. How that space is divided will, to some extent, be dictated by the location of utilities, particularly water, and also by function (most people will probably want a degree of privacy for sleeping and almost certainly for bathing) – but the potential is none the less enormous. Zoning for different activities allows us to examine exactly how we want to live and to use the space at our disposal. And our ideas about about this can change. At one time the kitchen was firmly located at the back of the house because it was where the servants worked, but as our lives at home have become less formal, the trend has been to open to open up the kitchen so that it becomes part of the living area.

Finding new uses for old buildings can revive ailing sites in the heart of great cities. At Butlers Wharf, by Tower Bridge on the south bank of London's River Thames, I was heavily involved in the first phase of the area's regeneration: a derelict 13-acre site is now home to the Design Museum, four of our restaurants and a mixed development of apartments, offices, shops and student accommodation. A little further upstream, the new Tate Gallery of Modern Art, in the converted Bankside power station, will continue the process of revitalizing south London. My experience at Butlers Wharf is not without its cautionary aspects, however. When we began work on the main riverfront warehouse, we discovered that it had been built without foundations, and rectifying the situation added hundreds of thousands of pounds to the budget.

As this book makes clear, the search for unusual spaces is not confined to the city: old agricultural barns and outbuildings, even an ice-cream factory, have been turned by ingenious individuals into homes of character and presence. What is it about these buildings that so appeals? Above all, I think, it is the potential to fashion a home as we want it to be, rather than to inherit a style imposed by previous occupants or – in the case of many new houses – the same dull look and configuration that planners and mass housebuilders insist we all want. *Converted Spaces* shows that we do not; it also opens our eyes to the liberating possibilities of making homes that respond to the way we live our modern lives.

TERENCE CONRAN

Half-title page: A wide-open loft space designed by architect Andrew Berman, New York City.

Title page: Wynkoop DuBois barn, Squibrocket, Martha's Vineyard.

Copyright and Contents page: Product designer Ross Lovegrove at home in his converted warehouse, London.

Opposite: The Anders Loft, New York City, designed by architects Kiss Cathcart Anders.

The post-industrial age dawned with electronic circuitry silently replacing the hiss and clank of moving parts. Factories and warehouses closed down as microchips and fibre-optic cables took over the work of machines. Changing demographics have emptied village schools and churches, and the leasing of farm machinery has freed up barns and sheds. In a world of shrinking resources, revitalizing such redundant buildings and turning them into homes offers city and rural dwellers the luxury of grand-scale space and exciting opportunities for creative self-expression – for those with the spirit to tackle them.

Originally a trend amongst artists seeking to create imaginative and practical living and working spaces, the conversion of abandoned buildings has grown into a worldwide phenomenon. People from all walks of life are now embracing the idea of converted living space. Imagine a living room the size of a factory floor with riverfront views, or a bedroom with a ceiling as high as a church vault, on the edge of an inner-city park. Imagine a kitchen as large as a telephone exchange, with a canal on one side and a supermarket on the other. The challenge is how to make these spaces liveable without losing their original character: they were never designed for human habitation.

The industrial fittings and fixtures of old printing works, flour mills, textile factories and barns can be removed, adapted or incorporated into domestic living spaces, but these buildings will not come equipped with creature comforts. Converting such sites for residential use automatically throws up questions of conservation and preservation. These days the buzz

① ② An empty barn in Pennsylvania or a vast warehouse will provide inspiration for those willing to experiment with open-plan living.

word for architects is 'contextual', as in 'appropriate', and stringent planning regulations exist to protect many of these buildings. In addition, some decisions like the siting of the kitchen or bathroom within an empty shell cannot be arbitrary, as they may be influenced by fire regulations or plumbing. The planning official will not question your furnishing style, but will need to ensure that building legislation is respected, so find out what the restrictions are before you embark upon renovations.

Furnishing a big, open living space requires a balance between complete freedom and existing constraints. The usual constraints of furniture, colour and pattern, and size and layout from room to room, do not exist in an open-plan converted space. Let the building suggest the furnishing style: country-house style in a factory loft, or even a barn, looks wrong and is more appropriate for a manor house. Domesticating a former industrial building is not a question of the old decorative stand-bys – carpet swatches, patterned fabrics and paint colours. Begin by considering the context within which you live and then impose your living habits upon all that space.

1 City Visions

A Sense of Place

'The very idea of someone leaving the centre of London to seek fame and fortune in a garden suburb just doesn't work, does it? And it's hard to believe that it ever will.' David Puttnam, film-maker and visionary on cities of the future, is metropolitan in his view. From the earliest times, urban communities have been the driving force behind human affairs. They remain irresistible destinations for all those who want to be where things are happening. At the turn of the century just 10 per cent of the global population lived in cities. Despite the Industrial Revolution, more people were engaged in agriculture than in manufacturing.

Now, a century later, over 50 per cent of the global population has migrated to the cities to find work, placing an even greater demand on space, and one that is partially met by the conversion of existing industrial structures to residential use.

Fifty years ago, industry needed buildings big enough to accommodate large-scale manufacturing machinery. And as little as twenty years ago, the mainframe computer for a moderately sized company would have had to be housed in a room as big as a ship's engine room. Now, computers with capacious memories and multiple software options can be carried on

board a plane or train as laptops no bigger than briefcases. The decline of heavy industry and the increased reliance of modern business on compact electronic circuitry have down-sized our need for gigantic office buildings and warehouse spaces. Now that their original function is obsolete, these structures are being reclaimed to provide residential space for the growing urban population.

Former factories and warehouses now make up some of the chicest urban addresses. Industrial buildings of past centuries were sited near transport facilities designed to receive raw materials, and many are located near the sea or beside canals. Converted to waterfront apartments, these buildings now command premium prices, and residents have the added advantages of not being overlooked by their neighbours and of benefiting from light reflecting off the water.

Some industrial buildings may be set in yards in which dray horses and carts were stabled.

❶ Stuart Parr knocked out 25m (82ft) of bricks from his New York loft to put in windows facing the Hudson River and Statue of Liberty.

❷ The view from an apartment in a converted city building is exhilaratingly different from the usual suburban prospect. This conversion in Islington, London, is surrounded by several centuries of architectural history.

Painter Julian Schnabel lives and paints in an old perfume factory in New York where the rings for horses' hay bags still adorn the walls of his apartment. He carried the drinking troughs up to the roof and planted them with flowers – a gesture that symbolizes the process of sympathetic adaptation that is the key to a successful conversion.

Loft-buying in converted industrial buildings is a familiar practice for city real-estate agents. By 'loft' they do not mean that area under the eaves accessed by foldaway stairs. Rather, 'loft' is the American term for an apartment within a former factory or warehouse. In the 1950s, Manhattan's cheap and unfashionable Soho lofts were colonized by artists for the exhibition of huge canvases and weighty bronzes that were easily supported by the reinforced-steel joists and concrete pillars. Later, in the 1970s, the artist's loft became a cult icon when Andy Warhol started filming in his notorious Factory.

Nowadays, in most urban industrial conversions, the property developers will already have fixed the roof, defined common parts, and supplied plumbing and electric services. Often, apartments are sold as shells with the side walls of the prospective home – those to be shared with neighbours – defined only by a single course of blocks. The layout of the rooms is left to the buyer, the only restriction being the position of the drains, which determine the site of the kitchen and the bathroom.

The skill in converting industrial space into residential apartments lies in making the building efficient and waterproof, and at the same time providing all the necessary services and allowing the individual owners to design their own interiors.

1 The vaulted shape of these elegant windows frames a view that the owners wanted to admire. The office opposite empties at night so they are not overlooked.

2 The building opposite these windows is on the diagonal, so privacy is assured.

3 The building adjacent to this apartment in New York overlooks the living area, so the owner slides a pair of curvaceous moulded screens by Alvar Aalto across the window.

Architect Piers Gough, who has brought to life a number of great buildings in London, calls it 'pre-washed, pre-shrunk architecture'. Much like a pair of Levi's 501s, such buildings are already classics. Within the bare shell the owner will decide whether to partition the spaces, how to make the most of natural light, and what colours and textures to add to complete the loft apartment.

The conquest of inner space within these cavernous warehouses and factories encourages adventurous people to band together in committees or housing associations to buy an unconverted property. In Nile Street, east London, nine residents pooled their resources to convert an empty warehouse into mixed living and working space, thus cutting out the property-developing middlemen. One of the housing association members, Jane Tankard, reveals that the project took two years to complete, and that the group risked everything on getting planning permission to mix residential space with working space. In the end it worked.

Although common walls and shared services make group action a necessity, working together can also be a matter of choice. Community is more than a shared garden and noise-abatement notices. Like the spirit and determination required to turn an empty warehouse or factory into a comfortable living space, it involves a shared attitude of mind.

Rural Landscapes

As changing farming methods empty agricultural buildings and the rural population gravitates to the cities, new inhabitants realize the potential to turn empty schools, churches and barns into dwellings. While we might refer to hard-edged industrial architecture as 'contextual' in the inner city, regional buildings in the country might be termed 'vernacular'. Any farm buildings converted for living space should retain the qualities of open space and the local materials, whether mellowed brick, old stone or wood.

Reluctant to live in a country house with the ghost of a vicar, interior decorator John Stefanidis transformed some derelict cowsheds into his country retreat. Throughout the conversion he used materials to fit in with the building traditions of the countryside. No precious woods have been used; the woodwork is pine, washed with white paint

mixed with a little ochre; the floor is brick and the walls are rough brick and plaster.

Every region has its own vernacular architecture. The solid stone arches, stuccoed walls and flagged floors of farmhouses in southern Spain; the cloistered grey-stone vaulted walkways and pergolas of

Tuscan villas; and the honeyed wooden cruck frames of barns in the British Midlands are all examples of different vernacular styles that use local materials and building styles. The search for authentic stone or old brick, or for the craftsman who can plaster with gesso or who can thatch, can be

1 At the end of the nineteenth century, as canals, roads and railroads brought rural communities closer to the newly industrialized cities, American country buildings were embellished with decorative devices. Here a weathered clapboard schoolhouse is highlighted by an ornate cupola. Dressed with gingerbread brackets it is more of a pavilion on top of the school, open on all sides with a view across woodlands. Not merely decorative, it increases light and ventilation, while the silhouette in the wintry landscape commands attention.

1

both expensive and fruitless – so contemporary solutions are sought. Mixing resin into cement will give it a burnish reminiscent of stone floors at half the expense. The architecture must be respected, however. Adding an ornate metal-and-glass conservatory onto a stone cottage, for example, would be brutal.

Rural buildings, like urban structures, offer large open spaces that can be divided or left open according to individual needs.

The constraints of farm buildings are as challenging to work around as shared walls or defunct warehouse lifts. Early American barns usually include one or more galleries on

either side of the threshing area, so living space arranged over a series of levels is a natural choice. Other features may be a porch on the building's broad side that protects the entrance with a projecting gable.

In most buildings that garner the harvest, there are no chimneys and, therefore, no hearth. Flue-cured

tobacco barns are the exception. While modernists in inner-city conversions salvage industrial radiators, wood-burning stoves are one of the joys of the countryside. But in wooden structures the addition of a fireplace is rarely successful, especially as flues and a chimney will have to be installed.

Similarly, the lack of windows in buildings that were not built to be inhabited is also a problem. In his long, narrow cowsheds, John Stefanidis put windows down both sides so that the rooms are suffused with cross-light. In a 200-year-old barn on a California wine estate, the owners made galleried walkways within the high, windowless barn walls. They placed the bedrooms like

Symbols of shelter and harvest, farm buildings convert into homes surrounded by fields.

1 Running water was never needed in a former tractor shed so rain barrels, painted to disappear into the horizon, collect rainwater now that the shed is a home.

2 **3** Built in 1894, this barn on Long Island, one of the largest of its type in the area, was used in dairy farming. In the 1950s white asbestos shingles were used to cover the exterior; these have recently been replaced with naturally weathered cedar shingles. The trapdoors in the floor were once used to deliver hay to the cows waiting below.

eyries under the high-pitched eaves and set skylights high in the A-frame pitched roof to beam in maximum light without spoiling the main fabric of the barn. Skylights may not be an option in cases where barn roofs – as well as other structural basics – are protected by conservation legislation that prevents owners from altering the building's exterior.

The 200-year-old barn in the California vineyard was once located in a different state. The 1780 pine structure was dismantled in New England and completely reassembled in California. The height of the barn was trimmed by 1.5m (4ft 11in), paned windows and a wooden cupola were added, and a walk-in fireplace of local serpentine rock was built.

British architect Richard Rogers told global strategists at the London School of Economics that cities in the next century will evolve like harbours, connected by electronic circuitry to other ports around the world. The same technology that has reduced the size of computer hardware (and the space needed to house it) allows more people the freedom to live outside the city and commute by computer link rather than by car. Country conversions need not be weekend retreats. A combined living and working space can be created in a rural barn as sympathetically as in an urban factory.

Preservation & Transformation

A Sense of Place

In any conversion, urban or rural, early decisions have to be made as to how much to cover up – or reveal – of a building's origins. Changes to the structure should be influenced by the building's history, yet sometimes authenticity is less important than individual style.

Preservationists get planning permission more easily than those proposing radical conversions, but adaptations within the original framework can transform buildings of no architectural distinction. Architect Michael Davis and

artist Andrew Logan received planning permission to renovate their 1950s garage on the condition that the extension required to turn it into an apartment, gallery and workshop matched the height of the existing building. The old garage doors were extended to become a 3.5sq.m (12½sq.ft) double doorway and were used to exhibit mirrored glass sculptures. Rather than puncturing the sides of the building, Davis and Logan installed a panelled glass roof from a garden centre, which gives them all the light that they require. They painted the walls orange and blue.

San Francisco architect William Leddy's conversion of a Pennsylvania barn celebrates vernacular architecture with 51cm (20in)-thick fieldstone walls and those vertical ventilation slots, typical of the area, called wind-eyes, which he enlarged and then glazed. The entrance to the narrow end of the barn is a new, galvanized, cylindrical steel silo that houses the upstairs bathroom for the main bedroom. Silos appeared on the American landscape in the 1930s and were used for the storage of grain for winter cattle food. Adding a new silo to give the inhabitants more space was inspired; the architect

Preserving the character of old workplaces in the town or country while adapting them to a new role as comfortable dwellings requires an early assessment of what to keep and what to replace.

1 Architect William Leddy extended a nineteenth-century stone barn near Philadelphia by erecting a new galvanized-steel silo at one end. Cattle-feed storage silos are a feature of the American rural landscape, but as this building no longer houses cattle and the owners needed a porch as well as an upper-level bathroom, this cylindrical tower has been given a contemporary function.

Some architectural details are worth keeping in any conversion, such as a priory window and door dating from the tenth and eleventh centuries. Cross-bracing and steel joists, pillars and posts, hardware, ducts and cogwheels that belong to a former industrial age are still talking points in the electronic one.

1 In architect George Whiteside's conversion of this factory in Toronto, the pipes running in horizontal and vertical directions automatically create divisions of space.

2 The decision to leave these vertical pipes exposed in Holley Loft, New York, inspired architects Hanrahan Meyers to echo their presence with pillars. In this expansive space, lighting has been used to define function.

was able to accommodate current living needs while observing a rural building tradition.

A young couple in the Australian outback ignored the niceties of preservation. Alex Willcock and Sophie Conran's old, window-less tractor shed lacked any of the conveniences of modern-day living. They punched holes in the corrugated iron walls and placed second-hand wooden windows in the gaps. They also built a huge fireplace. 'We had a complete blank canvas with no history, no garden and we wanted to make it look as if we had been there a long time.'

In any conversion, decisions have to be made about conceal-ments and disguises, exposure and exaggeration, as well as what to preserve and what to discard. Architects, by the nature of their training, tend to be in favour of letting the roots show through. However, not all of them subscribe to the approach

that leaves the building's service pipes exposed. In a conversion be architect John Beckmann, a New York loft in an old paint factory has clusters of pipes concealed behind light-grey plasterboard inset between the original pillars. Respecting the building's past means being aware of inconsistencies and allowing the building to dictate the form of the conversion but not constrain it.

This compromise between preser-vation and new construction was also achieved in a Melbourne malthouse. Since 1907 the space has been dominated by a copper vat once used for storing hops. When the malthouse was eventually divided into apartments, interior designer Michelle Harrington built around the vat, leaving its verdigris coppery drum partially exposed in the new brickwork to remind residents of the building's history. Its rounded, cylindrical shape inspired other aspects of the design, including the porthole windows, which were inset into the

cement walls. Even the bilge
pump, newly polished, remains in
the foyer as a conversation piece
for the building in its new role.

Artifice without artificiality
is a skill that architects exhibit
in many conversions. In a former
1930s tractor shed, Australian
architect Glenn Murcutt decided
to keep the corrugated iron
roof and its tallow-wood
walls but threw out practically
everything else. An enclosed
Victorian verandah was removed
and the new verandah roof
pitched upwards instead of down,
so that it resembled wing flaps.
The high roof spaces were given

Not all decisions to preserve or radically alter
space have to be structural – they can be as
simple as choosing a furnishing style.

1 In a former nineteenth-century bank the
fluted column and large, arched windows
inspired period furnishings as carefully
assembled as a theatre set. Owned by
New York photographers David McDermott
and Peter McGough, the bank has been
restored and furnished to reflect their
dedication to living in the past. The Homburg
hat and the goldfish bowl are inspired.

2 In this former paint factory in Brussels the
glass mansard roof suggested the conservatory-
style furniture, while a chandelier belies the
room's industrial origins.

3 Flagstone floors and vaulted entrances in
St. Symphorien Priory in south-east France are
enhanced by simple furnishings that complement
the building's unspoilt beauty.

double windows at each end that pull back to ventilate the entire shed. In Murcutt's approach, newly constructed features, like the stainless-steel kitchen, are visually distinguished from the original structure, but not rough-cut and hewn to replicate the original as if in a theme park.

Finding a balance between respecting the building's past and the theme-park approach is something that Australian builder Wayne Cross sought to achieve in his 1940s veterinary-supply factory in Melbourne. To do this he rendered the architraves to give them the patina of age and then tinted the original wooden floors brick-red to introduce a more modern, industrial look. A corrugated-steel kitchen behind sliding glass doors, which replaced the original cross-barred factory doors, is a contemporary addition, while the existing loading area has been glazed to turn it into an atrium.

Conversions by their nature impose new elements onto old structures. The very best conversions are those in which the architectural heritage is respected by the new inhabitants, who allow the

overall style to be dictated by its form. This need not stifle creativity. A monumental neo-classical bank in London suggested an Italian palazzo to its owners, Philip and Carol Thomas. So they staged a dramatic trans-formation by opening out the former public banking area into a series of living rooms, creating a *piano nobile* beneath high ceilings.

Just as the constraints of a building and planning guidelines limit what changes can be made, they can also trigger imaginative solutions. To revitalize existing spaces without losing their historic appeal is the aim of any thoughtful conversion.

1 Freedom of Expression

A Sense of Place

One of the great liberating aspects of any conversion in the town or country is the vast open space – none of it divided by doors, intersected with corridors or partitioned into rooms. Mezzanines, shower cubicles and kitchen workstations become their surrogates, opening up a wide range of possible configurations. Strong enough to impose a style, the architecture of these buildings also allows a freedom of expression that more conventional, purpose-built buildings inhibit.

The appeal of these spaces is so great that many of the converted have given up an entire way of life to start again. As children grow up there is a noticeable trend for couples to move out of their overstuffed town or country houses and sell their possessions. Then they convert an industrial or agricultural building and admire their new-found freedom. Science writer Ian Tarr spent 17 years in the suburbs of London before he tired of commuting to his Georgian terraced (row) house. He sold it, together with the entire contents, and bought an empty shell within a loft conversion in London's Soho. His brief to his architect Nico Rensch was 'uncluttered simplicity', and he now lives in a Zen-like open space, divided only by sliding polycarbonate screens.

The freedom of expression that these huge buildings allow often

inspires the inhabitant to try something entirely new. The owner of a Scottish castle – furnished in true baronial style with suits of armour and high-backed dark-wood chairs – started again when he commissioned architects Sally Mackreth and James Wells to furnish his loft in

① Beneath the insulated and pitched roof of an industrial building, daylight is screened. Curtained-off space can be fun to light at night: fluorescent tube-lights evenly illuminate this space, while at ground level there are temporary, but amusing and playful, light sculptures.

② Large open spaces encourage all sorts of free-wheeling action. One American architect even calls the central core of his open loft space 'the piazza'. Here, the huge gymnasium in an old schoolhouse conversion retains its original floor markings, and makes an excellent children's playground.

London with uncluttered lines and modern furniture. They lined the walls of a washroom with lilac suede and added a stainless-steel ceiling.

The right attitude of mind and a pioneering spirit are all you need. People who live in these converted spaces never live life on the fringes. They are either in the heart of the city or deep in the country. In the country they can hear the owl hoot at night, and actually see the stars. They browse in local markets, garner home-grown produce and breathe fresh air. In the city, residents go to work on in-line rollerblades, watch chalk-artists at work on the pavements and get their Sunday papers on Saturday. Whatever the scenario, these people have an insider's view of life. Suburbia is a lifetime away.

The freedom of expression that space inspires in residential conversions can be just as liberating in public buildings. Vast factories that once housed industrial workers and machines have been brought back to life in new roles as recreational spaces. Theatres, art galleries, shops, hotels, restaurants, clubs and designer studios are now opening in empty banks, post offices, telephone exchanges and printworks.

The successful transformation of industrial spaces into places for pleasure and leisure is a result of the vision and inventiveness of the architects and town planners, and also of theatre directors, set designers and gallery curators within the public domain. Without a proscenium, directors and producers can involve the audience in theatrical events as scenes unfold around them. Without sequential rooms opening out one from another, curators of museum collections or of paintings and sculpture discover new ways of revealing works of art.

Faced with the grand proportions of former industrial buildings, architects have to think on an awesome scale. Their skill lies in turning potential disadvantages — a lot of artificial light, and poor acoustics — into advantages. So the cloistered, semi-dark interior of a derelict bus depot in Manchester, England, has been turned to positive effect in its new role as a textile museum. The building now houses centuries-old examples of fabric from Manchester's spinning mills, which need to be humidified and, more importantly, protected from too much natural light.

Factories and warehouses built to support heavy machinery, with load-bearing walls and floors, steel or concrete beams and columns, can easily support theatre scenery. In New York, Shakespeare is performed in a former library at the Joseph Papp

theatre; while in Paris, a former munitions factory, the Cartouche de Vincennes, offers fireworks of a different kind in its theatrical productions.

The sheer scale of these grand buildings draws clubbers as well as theatre audiences, and inner-city warehouses play music all night at house parties. Fashion designer Donna Karan held the launch party for her London flagship store in a gigantic warehouse, furnishing the cavernous, grey concrete building with salvaged railway sleepers (ties) for benches and tables, dressing them in white linen, with orchids and porcelain. Shops and restaurants on an awesome scale also occupy such spaces as these.

Observing the changing role of these former workplaces is an exciting prospect as it regenerates urban areas, but it can also be an emotional experience for the residents of a city who have witnessed the demise of industry. In 1990, when the Scottish city Glasgow, was awarded the title European City of Culture, Bill Dryden staged a play there, inspired by the closure of the shipyards. In a derelict yard, set designer Bill Dudley built the steel ribs of a liner's hull to accommodate both set and seating. At the climax of the play, art imitated life as the timber supports were freed, and the final 'liner' slipped its moorings to slide into the water, leaving most of the audience in tears.

1 2 Photographer Fabrizio Ferri's Industria complexes, located in New York and Milan, are multi-purpose former industrial buildings used, among other things, for exhibitions and catwalk shows.

Museums & Galleries

A generation of conceptual artists, which began with the Arte Povera in Italy in the late 1960s, suffered from a lack of adequate space to exhibit their work. In response to this, spatial volumes were realized in brick and stone, creating galleries on a scale that would have been unthinkable in the nineteenth- and early twentieth-centuries.

At the Henry Moore Studio at Dean Clough, a former textile mill in Halifax, Yorkshire, the conversion of a seven-storeyed, 37m (120ft)-high Victorian carpet factory has given sculptors and artists the space to create bold work. Originally required to take the weight of the carpet looms, the floors were built to support as much as 1 ton per sq.ft. Often, loading bays and giant double doors – even cranes and fork-lifts – in former industrial spaces make the installation of works of art simpler. Richard Long fork-lifted 15 tons of coal into the studio for one of his magical circles, while German sculptor Ulrich Rückriem created his huge monoliths out of the local York stone.

The amount of wall space in such buildings, unbroken by partition walls and corridors, is an obvious advantage for hanging and viewing works of art. The Musée d'Orsay in Paris, which was originally built as a train station for the Exposition Universelle of 1900, now houses paintings and sculpture, including a collection of Impressionist paintings. In a smaller but equally intriguing conversion, Spain's leading museum of modern art, the Reina Sofia, has found a new home in a converted hospital in Madrid.

Art gallery conversions are exacting since even the doors and windows can make or break the fluidity of the space. The vertiginous heights of an abandoned power station at Bankside, London, would not seem to be the friendliest show-case for sculpture and paintings. The Tate Gallery's decision to acquire this building for its modern art collection was based on the exciting dynamics offered by the huge spaces. As the Director of the Tate, Nicholas Serota, has pointed out, there is an increasing tendency for some artists to involve the physical space of a gallery or museum in their work. He quoted sculptor Carl Andre on the evolution of sculpture in the twentieth century as a change of interest from 'sculpture as form' to 'sculpture as structure' and finally to 'sculpture as place'.

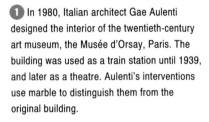

❶ In 1980, Italian architect Gae Aulenti designed the interior of the twentieth-century art museum, the Musée d'Orsay, Paris. The building was used as a train station until 1939, and later as a theatre. Aulenti's interventions use marble to distinguish them from the original building.

❷ The Henry Moore Studio at Dean Clough, the former carpet-weaving mill, is an imposing space for Richard Long's installation, *Halifax Circle* (1989), in Delabole slate.

Donald Judd, the American sculptor and painter, created a new form of museum at Marfa, Texas, in a cluster of abandoned military buildings and World War II aircraft hangars. Large permanent installations of his own and other artists' work are housed in the hangars, quarter-masters' stores, the armoury and in adobe-style additions. The main purpose of the museum is the permanent installation of art within the space, since Judd believes that 'museums are at best anthologies'. Change is brought about not by new juxtapositions, but by the changing environment – natural light and weather conditions – and the changing perspective of the viewer.

Another gallery conversion is the Hallen für Neue Kunst in Schaffhausen, Switzerland, where modern art is housed in a former textile factory. Here artists' works are presented as clusters, creating the effect of overlapping and merging zones of creativity, drawing together artists of the same generation and related sensibilities. As at Marfa, the aim is for a more interactive relationship between the viewer and the work viewed. The object of the curator is to surround the viewer with powerful juxtapositions of art, rather than giving an encyclopaedic, art historian's tour.

A hundred years ago galleries aimed to educate people through a series of rooms housing chronologically ordered collections. Today things have changed, and museums and galleries now celebrate the open, fluid spaces of converted buildings that allow viewers to experience art more fully. Like the buildings themselves, the collaborations of living and dead artists promote a dialogue between past and present.

Theatres & Clubs

A Sign of the Times

Why does a factory often make a better theatre than any other place? With the right direction, vast open spaces, without tiered seating or a proscenium and wings, encourage participation by an audience in the performance.

For the last thousand years European theatres have been built along the same lines and to much the same size. A Shakespearean theatre or a Veronese courtyard theatre, a Paris music hall or a

Theatrical buildings can play a part in theatrical events. Unpretentious, high-roofed sheds that once housed trams or shipbuilding works have gantries on high levels and tremendous floor space, so that far more audience participation is possible. Directors manipulate this space, borrowing methods from film production rather than live theatre.

1 The Tramway in Glasgow before the shed was converted.

2 **3** The Catalan group, La Fura dels Baus, perform in the Tramway theatre after its conversion. The audience circulates freely in the open space around the set.

Berlin club, all share the same dimensions: horseshoe galleries set above a pit-like space in the middle and with the stage beyond. The system is designed to keep the audience in their seats and the actors distanced upon the stage. Until now.

Now empty industrial spaces inspire a fertile artistic imagination. In the 1960s, architect Sir Denys Ladsun suggested at a planning meeting that theatre director Peter Brook would prefer a bombed site in Brixton to anything that he, Ladsun, could design. Brook agreed. He is famous for his peripatetic

performances around the world, and likes to stage these in what he calls 'found' spaces not designed for theatrical performances.

When the trams stopped running in Glasgow, the vast tram shed in the centre of the city that once housed them became derelict, and it was not until the 1990s that the site was reclaimed with grants given to develop public spaces. The new Tramway theatre sited there was inaugurated with a Peter Brook production of the *Mahabharata*, one of the great epic poems of ancient India, which was ideally suited to such a space. Without theatrical flats and stages, let alone orchestra pits and tiers of seating, there were no boundaries to cross as firewalkers performed in one section and lines were delivered by performers in another. The audience, seated in clusters on the floor, but able to wander at will, could become part of the performance in the great ebb and flow of the epic.

As well as encouraging audience participation, conversions of industrial buildings with giant proportions can have a great impact on the creative energy unleashed. In Hamburg, Germany, the Kampnagelfabrik ('Factory theatre') has become one of the most famous alternative theatres in Europe. Housed in a crane factory, built in 1875, and later used as an armaments factory in World War II, it was converted into a theatre space in 1981. In summer the gigantic flat roof is illuminated by lights rigged to gantries high enough for bungee jumping, as an open-air ballet takes place there, before a sky-high audience.

These examples illustrate the creative potential of former industrial buildings as a backdrop for artistic programmes. Dramatist Arianne Mnouchkine, who set up her theatre in a munitions factory in Paris, sums up the attraction of these conversions: 'Because the Cartouche de Vincennes has been

built to house creations, productions, works, inventions and explosions, it is a neutral, empty space, but an inspiring empty space that can be filled with images.' It involves the audience directly in the creative act of theatre.

Old warehouses and factories are being opened to another more adventurous group – clubbers. These clubs open and close as fast as hemlines rise and fall, and only the most rudimentary changes are made to the industrial spaces in terms of surfaces and furnishings. Rather, this generation of clubbers participates in a pulsating, vibrant atmosphere of sound and light with coloured laser shows and dynamic sound systems. Such a place is the Café Flèche d'Or in Paris. Housed in an old train station in the 20th *arrondissement*, it offers a journey through a time-tunnel of noise and sound. The Hacienda, once Manchester's most notorious club, was sited in a former factory. Here grimy brick walls became the background for metallic spray-painted signs, while traffic bollards (posts) demarcated the dance floor from walkways. Other nightclubs that flourished in the 1980s included the techno-dance studio Test Department, which was situated in an abandoned train roundhouse beneath a London flyover (road bridge). Within this enormous iron structure over 1,000 people met to dance the night away. Rising 3m (10ft) up in

the centre of the building, a round stage was transformed into a platform for the dancers, with the central column emblazoned with the slogan 'The unacceptable face of freedom'. Even the sculptures by Malcolm Poynter and London's Mutoid Waste Collective were made from recycled, industrial waste – panels, barrels, coils, junk metal and heavy rope nets – thereby continuing a theme of transformation. In the country these dance clubs are more nomadic, often no more than one-night stands held in empty farm-machinery sheds. However, the same principles apply, with lighting riggers and sound-system technicians over-scaling everything to beam out a wall of light and sound to match the enormity of the space.

The theatricality of these vast abandoned buildings can be used for all manner of entertainment experiences. The spatial freedom encourages – and easily accommodates – the large numbers of people that such events draw, while also inspiring audacious effects.

▶ The Café Flèche d'Or in Paris is a fashionable nightclub in an old train station. Mosaic floors and dado rails, and the original high-ceilinged walls and grilles, lit with a battery of coloured lights, are used with considerable inventiveness.

2 Restaurants, Shops & Hotels

A Sign of the Times

As the hours spent in offices decrease worldwide, leisure time doubles. The working week, which in the United Kingdom was 60 hours at the start of the twentieth century, has been reduced to an average of 40 hours. Today we spend only one-third of our lives at work, and many industrial workplaces have now been turned into leisure space, for shopping, dining or visiting as tourists.

Restaurants designed in warehouses and factories are able to accommodate a large number of people. Terence Conran, who began his successful series of restaurants with Bibendum, housed in a former Michelin tyre depot, pioneered the idea of converting industrial spaces into modern restaurants. Some of these seat several hundred diners and some also incorporate specialist food shops on an awesome scale. Amongst these is The Bluebird Garage, first opened in 1923 in Chelsea, London. By the 1950s it was being used as an ambulance station, and later it became a fashion market. Inspired by its grandeur – a mixture of classical, neo-Georgian and Art Deco – Conran chose it as the site for his spectacular restaurant and food market. Today the garage forecourt boasts a steel-and-glass canopy for the outdoor fruit and vegetable market; the 650sq.m (7,000sq.ft) ground-floor space sites specialist counters for meat, fish, oils and spices, dairy products, pastas and confectionary, as well as a café, a

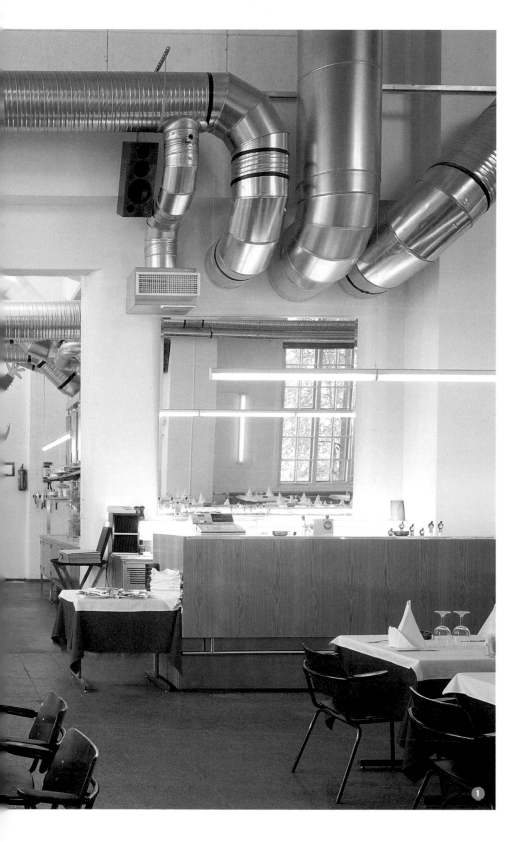

1 This utilitarian restaurant in Helsinki once housed telecommunications company Nokia.

2 The Waag in Amsterdam is named to recall the building's history as a goods-weighing warehouse.

flower market and a chef's shop; and situated in the 9m (30ft)-high, nave-like first-floor interior is a restaurant and seafood bar. Conran's other London ventures include Quaglino's, located in the former 1920s Quaglino's Restaurant, and Le Pont de la Tour in a warehouse overlooking Tower Bridge.

Another conversion of a derelict shell into a fashionable address for dining is the chic top-floor restaurant, owned by the department store Harvey Nichols, in the old OXO building, a familiar London

landmark on the River Thames. The building has kept its distinctive portholes, as well as a signature X-shaped window, which graphically announce the name of the beef extract malted there in the 1930s when cargo ships still came up the Thames.

Designers have been quick to recognize the potential of huge buildings in prime inner-city sites. Romeo Gigli acquired the unlikely premises of a former abattoir in the heart of Paris in order to turn it into a new boutique for fantasy clothes, and Paul Smith opened his first fashion shop in London's Covent Garden in an old post office. He discovered the place of his dreams by shining his flashlight through the mail box one night and finding the big, open space he needed. From such simple beginnings his empire has grown to 200 shops across the globe and a turnover of some £142 million a year. Photographer Fabrizio Ferri built

his retailing business in Italy around the warehouses and factories of Milan, as well as acquiring a parking garage in New York which he turned into studios, attracting supermodels, famous photographers and the inevitable paparazzi. The next step was to launch his Industria collection of clothing and restaurants within these spacious venues. Having developed a taste for giving historic buildings a new lease of life, Ferri also opened a hotel, the Monasterio, on a volcanic Italian island called Pantelleria. The hotel is built around a cluster of old *dammusi*, the island's characteristic domed-roof stone huts where monks once lived.

Hotel accommodation in a century-old water tower in Cologne – the cylindrical Hotel im Wasserturm – has been designed by Andrée Putman. The building had to be segmented like an orange into rooms radiating out from the central lobby on each floor. The colour of the original bricks and the repetitive arches inspired the mellow colour scheme inside, as well as the half-moon leitmotiv of the hotel. Backlit, water-green glass in the hotel bar and bathrooms reinforces the watery theme.

No one embraces the cool, contemporary style in converted buildings more enthusiastically than New York-based hotelier Ian Schrager. Having conquered

Miami, Los Angeles and New York with the most fashionable hotels in the United States – fitted out by two French designers, Andrée Putman and Philippe Starck – Schrager has found four new sites in London, including a former post office, a shop, and a warehouse belonging to the fabric retailer Sanderson. He has commissioned Starck (who designed the all-white Delano Hotel in Miami, and the Royalton and Paramount in New York) to transform them into modern hotels.

The enthusiasm for revamping industrial buildings, and the courage of the people who convert them, have brought about innovative contemporary design. As links between the past and forward-looking enterprises, these buildings nod to the conservationist attitude of the 1990s while being the evangelists for direct, modern, liveable design. Designers, theatre directors, museum curators, hoteliers and restaurateurs, as well as residents, are now approaching unused industrial buildings with a hopeful eye.

Printworks, Paris

The best of all eras

When new technology forced the closure of a printing factory in a small street near the Seine in the 6th *arrondissement* of Paris, French interior designer Andrée Putman bought the entire top floor and rooftop terrace. Internationally renowned for her work in hotels such as Morgans in New York and Im Wasserturm in Cologne, she has also designed fashion shops for Azzedine Alaïa and Karl Lagerfeld, as well as the Centre d'Art museum of Bordeaux. Her interiors unite modern lines and materials with French design of the 1930s and 40s, when the International Style introduced streamlined geometry. Her favoured materials include wood and straw, shagreen and linen, all in a palette of neutral, natural tones. Her roots may be in the French Moderne, but her poised and elegant interpretation of it half a century later are thoroughly modern.

For 18 years, Andrée lived in a seventeenth-century building on the opposite side of the street to the printing factory. She admits that the move from a period building into a late-nineteenth-century industrial loft felt like a divorce. But with her unerring instinct for the contemporary, she now lives in one of the most fashionable apartments in Paris. As her own designer and architect, her brief was very open: 'Leave it empty, with islands of objects and art, and make this woman feel happy and free.'

First she installed a window-wall within the open-plan living area of 150sq.m (1,615sq. ft), facing west. The window-wall does not block the daylight that bathes the apartment, but does create divisions within the living space. The wall stops before the end of the apartment to create a light-filled L-shape. Hidden when you enter the open living area (3), it is noticeable only from the middle of the room. Original cast-iron columns allow her to distance the sleeping space at night by pulling across screens made of fibreglass, which she calls her mosquito net. Behind the glass wall is the bathing space (4). Lace curtains dating from the beginning of the nineteenth century allow her to open or close the view, 'so that when I bathe I see the entire space – trees on one side and the paintings inside my apartment on the other.' The glass panes of the window in the new wall, framed in steel, reproduce exactly the existing garden-elevation windows.

Andrée's kitchen is in the greenhouse on her rooftop terrace (6), reached by stairs. A very good cook, she likes to entertain in different locations. Flexibility has always been important to her; she has never liked rooms and closed doors. She prefers to pull up the right number of chairs and eat wherever the mood takes her. In the main living room are eight metal chairs, designed in 1938 by Jacques-Emile Ruhlmann, and an elegant table by Paul Dupré-Lafon, dated 1935. In the kitchen, a table with an enamelled smoke-blue lava top on a metal Directoire foot offers a more intimate setting; while out on the adjoining rooftop terrace, old steel and grey marble café tables cluster for outdoor dining under the stars. With each change of location there is a change of pace and mood. The designer says, 'I try to be downstairs but my family and friends love to be upstairs to get the birdsong.'

One of the surprises in the immaculately conceived makeover was that the terrace has provided a microclimate which makes it possible to grow plants from Provence.

'I use a mix of objects to emphasize lines'
ANDRÉE PUTMAN

'Although I had no planning problems, one of my neighbours became ill with jealousy because of my garden,' Andrée recalls.

Like all modernists, Andrée Putman peels away the artifice to get to the heart of a building, to emphasize what is already there. She says her attitude towards design has been influenced by her own appearance, which she uses to exaggerate line and form. Being tall, she goes taller with very high heels, her broad athletic shoulders highlighted with a well-cut jacket. 'So I use a mix of objects to emphasize lines.'

Her move to a bigger, more fluid open space encouraged a rigorous paring down of her possessions. So emphatic is her belief that the walls should be free from intrusion that she reduced her contemporary art collection to a few favourites.

There were two skylights that offered views onto the rooftop terrace. To draw in more light, she made these much bigger, and kept the window treatments simple. Because she values the quality of light, she used large linen panels which slide vertically to one side, or go up and down like Roman blinds. The white walls reflect this light, as do the polished concrete floors, finished with a resin that creates a burnished background. Big round rugs make conversation areas in the open space and define the sitting areas. Daylight is balanced by what Andrée Putman calls 'an amazing array' of small sources of artificial light. There are 14 lamps in the big room and four in the bathroom, including one wall

sconce, two glass lights suspended from the ceiling, and a light illuminating the Eileen Gray mirror. Slim-profiled electric radiators are unobtrusive and efficient heaters in the main living room. In the small, A-frame, glazed conservatory kitchen on the roof, heating is not a problem. In fact, the kitchen has been air-conditioned.

There are very few pieces of furniture. Andrée Putman says that experience has taught her to respect – and find – the best of all the eras, yet always have an important space for what is new and beautiful. Classic furniture resolves its differences with contemporary pieces, all chosen for their elegance and poise as much as their timelessness: a desk in ebony and ivory dating

PLAN: Arrow in blue denotes roof terrace
Upper-level kitchen detail (2) not shown on plan

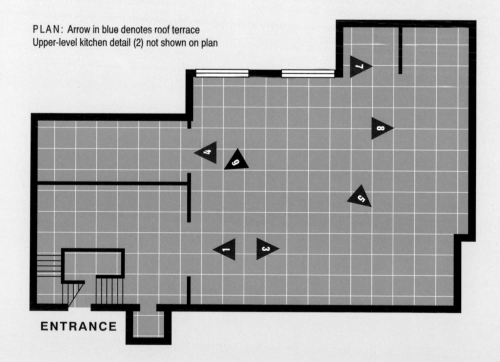

ENTRANCE

to the 1930s, a Louis XIV-era Boulle commode, and the Ruhlmann chairs. The colours are subdued: black, ivory and silver, with rugs in natural cream and sofas in white linen. The space is enlivened by the few modern paintings Andrée allowed to accompany her on this new adventure: by Van Velde, Schnabel, Alechinsky, Pincemin, Garouste and Boltanski. 'I don't use colour much since colour comes with life, from the flowers, the plates, the people's sweaters,' she says.

If you need to ask what style is, then you don't have it – a harsh truism of the impatient *fin-de-siècle* set. Andrée Putman's inspired melding of the classic and the contemporary is the nearest we can come to codifying her style. She believes that style is such an elusive quality that when sought, it vanishes without trace. Ecart, the name of her interior design and furnishing business in Paris, is trace spelled backwards. Now she is no longer at the helm, having sold the business. She says that to develop style, you have to kill that paralysing respect for period authenticity and images of wealth. Responsible for the revival of early twentieth-century designs at Ecart, Andrée Putman is now directing us towards the future, promoting flexibility and self-expression, and freedom from the dictates of style.

As the world shrinks in the slipstream of jet travel, we have begun to re-evaluate space as the most important commodity we can buy. In Japan, where land values are among the highest in the world, apartments are measured by the standard dimensions of tatami mats. In the West, space has been more plentiful, yet we have carved it up into rooms, boxes within boxes, stuffed full of our possessions, minimizing floor space and mistaking claustrophobia for cosiness.

The fullness of an empty space is one of those fashionable minimalist concepts that is hard to wrap your head around if you cannot visualize the potential of acres of white space. In truth, the first glimpse of all that space within the empty shell of a huge derelict loft or barn can be daunting.

Artist and craftsman Donald Judd described proportion as 'reason made visible'. Good proportions often disappear in the conversion of a warehouse or factory; but a vast steel beam lowering floor-to-ceiling height or an entrance with an overscaled door can be resolved either by making structural changes or through interior design. Building a gallery, or adding a new ceiling or raised floor can disguise undesirable proportions, as can cleverly placed accessories. Mirrors in unexpected places can create an impression of space as well as enhancing light by bouncing it back.

Not only do conversions offer large empty spaces that need to be shaped into different functional areas, they also include intrusive common parts – immovable pillars, ramps or joists – which may take a bite out of what would otherwise be a rectangular apartment. The skill is to compensate structurally for missing chunks, and then cover up any flaws with furnishings.

① **②** Architect Piers Gough's plans to make loft space within this former rock 'n' roll club in Soho, London, are in contrast to the famous Japanese capsule hotel, which offers economically priced cubicles.

One way of dealing with the vast floor-to-ceiling heights in factories and farm buildings is to install mezzanines or galleried walkways. These split levels have encouraged some of the most inventive staircases since the days of Busby Berkeley in Hollywood, from simple fire-escape designs to staircases made of steel mesh and rigged like yachts with halyards.

The natural light will have to be balanced with light fixtures. Factories and warehouses, milking sheds and flour mills were often artificially lit by day, and are built on a scale that leaves the inner core dim. Natural and artificial light need to be manipulated for residential use. Ingenious solutions have been developed to allow light to filter into dark recesses – such as skylights in top-floor apartments or barns.

As important as light are the acoustics. Rooms help to contain noise, which is why open-plan living can turn a space into an echo chamber. Surface materials on floors, walls and ceilings help to absorb sound, as do soft furnishings.

Whether you have a modern apartment in a warehouse building or a rustic barn conversion, decisions as to how the space is divided, lit and furnished must be made at the stage when the property is just an architectural shell.

The Architectural Shell

Space & Proportion

The Architectural Shell

From the outside, many potential loft-apartment conversions look like handsome, reassuringly solid, mellowed-brick buildings. The inside might seem unfamiliar territory. Whatever happened to the entrance hall? Or corridors leading off rooms? Is that a bedroom on a galleried mezzanine floor? And why are there so few doors?

The wonderful thing about buying an industrial space that was never designed with rooms in mind, is that the choice of dividing up the space and playing with proportions is up to each individual owner.

Architect Piers Gough explains how some property developers divide up former industrial space into manageable, habitable units and install services without too much disruption. 'Loft living is the modern alternative and we act as the enabler. Taking a specific building with a spirit and quality of its own, we then act with minimal intervention. We want to reveal the building rather than transform it, and to allow the owner the thrill of the space and the environment.'

The thrill of the space can be somewhat limited by the building's industrial past. Concrete walls strong enough to house a printing factory may resist being clad in something new; rafters made of reinforced steel beams that

1 In the Pattern House by Arthur Collin Architects, the high, ducted ceilings are brought down to a more human scale with the introduction of partition walls and a screen behind the modern sofa.

2 Low partitions also play a part in this garage conversion in Deptford, London. Architect Mark Guard removed all the horizontal joists supporting the original roof to create a large space on the first floor, which is now the main living room.

crisscross like road junctions, or awkward corners that once held heavy machinery, may be difficult to work into a residential plan. Some architects will incorporate existing constraints into the new plan. For example, the copper silo in Michelle Harrington's design for a former malthouse in Melbourne was lovingly restored, and the integral bilge pumps adjoining it were left

to provide a talking point in what is now the entrance hall for an apartment complex.

Developers often commission an interior designer to design a 'show' space to help prospective buyers envisage the building's potential.

1 Catalan architect Ricardo Bofil lives in the ruins of a cement factory that is not sized for family life. Its awesome proportions are heightened by tall, arched entrances, while large rugs delineate areas for sitting on the floor.

2 Where there are no rooms, screens can help define proportions. In this New York City loft the architects Dean/Wolf highlighted a slender column with a freestanding yellow room divider.

3 A solid block of colour applied to the wall, with an easel-like frame propped against it to support an abstract painting, helps to make this room's proportions less intimidating.

For commercial reasons show spaces are usually the meanest in the block. Looking beyond the decorative camouflage of floor and wall coverings, kitchen units and bathroom tiles, one can get a sense of how space and proportion can be modified. The location of windows, for example, affects the position of the bedroom and seating areas; the siting of kitchens and bathrooms will be restricted by the position of drains and available plumbing.

The shape of an apartment in a big building may be unconventional. Industrial features like chutes, or gigantic lifts that cannot be removed, take an awkward bite out of the space that will have to be worked into the plan. Safety regulations must also be observed. In Britain you cannot site stairs anywhere near a window; banisters have a specified width and must be a certain distance apart; and there must be fire exits and fire doors between working, living and communal areas.

When architectural shells are sold as apartments, all you will find at the outset are the four walls and the front door, with all the services – gas, electricity and water – capped off. Building controls vary in different countries so it is sensible at this stage to seek the advice of an architect and a structural engineer who will be able to configure the space according to your needs and the building regulations.

There is a lot of room for individual preferences in the spatial manipulation. Minimalist architect Claudio Silvestrin asks 'Why live in a series of boxes within one big box?' His ideal client requires only a door to the bathroom and maybe another to a baby's room; in fact, he has been commissioned by a developer to remodel a London house from three bedrooms to two, a reflection of the commercial value of space and light over room count.

Buildings that were never originally designed for habitation are a challenge to bring into satisfying proportions. Proportion refers to the spatial dimensions – the height of the ceiling in comparison with the width of the floor, the size of the windows and the doors. While a warehouse diminishes its occupants, a schoolhouse scaled to the size of children might give the inhabitant the sensation of being

exposed two of the original arched windows. To make better use of this high space he added a minstrel's gallery, which is reached by a nineteenth-century French oak staircase.

A sense of proportion is also affected by the use of furnishings. Adjusting the scale of furniture in vast buildings allows you to accentuate – or disguise –the volume of the space. Artist James Brown, who set up his family home within a former hotel in New York, inherited double-height, two-tiered windows that gave the space a vertical line. Big, comfortable wing chairs and other overscaled early modern pieces – from Adolf Loos and Josef Hoffmann to early Art Deco – in great blocks of colour, help to balance the vertiginous heights and take the eye horizontally across the window line-up.

Alice in Wonderland. Assembly halls, gyms and classrooms are spacious, but banisters at knee-height for adults, and door handles too far down to reach without bending, will need to be altered. Sometimes, changes in scale are surprising: in his conversion of an English country schoolhouse, Graham Carr kept the waist-high deep-bowl washbasins in the cloakroom. More extensive work was needed in the large assembly hall, where he removed a false ceiling – inserted to save on heating bills – and

exaggerate what she perceived as disadvantages. Her learning curve began with herself. Believing that her shoulders were too broad, she accentuated them further with padded jackets; thinking her legs were too long, she wore stilettos. Naturally, when she exchanged her Paris apartment for a vast space, she accentuated the vastness, paring down her furniture and allowing space and light to dominate her plan.

1 French architect Gilles Bouchez has introduced the concept of a house within a factory. His new structure containing the kitchen and bedrooms has been built with minimal alteration to the factory building.

2 The arched windows suggested the shape of this internal structure, which runs diagonally within a Rhode Island loft conversion by Boston architects Peter Forbes and Associates.

3 A purposeful gap created in a curved wall separating the living area from the kitchen exposes a complicated arrangement of factory pipes.

4 The Belgian owners of this former school hall introduced a new partition wall with three elegantly proportioned doors for their open-plan living space.

Standard-size doors will diminish a grand entrance in a vast open space, which is why architects often specify ceiling-to-floor doors. Details that accentuate the architecture are vital in correcting proportions. For centuries interior designers have played with scale, adding dado rails or detailed cornices and mouldings to raise or lower the apparent floor-to-ceiling height. A conversion's equivalent of the dado rail is tongue-and-groove panelling reaching two-thirds of the way up the wall, which helps to give a space a more human scale.

If the focal point of a room is double doors, or a panel of windows framing a view of the city, it can be balanced with symmetrical seating areas on either side. French interior designer Andrée Putman once revealed that the secret of her style was to

Windows

As Steen Rasmussen points out in *Experiencing Architecture*, 'The same room can be made to give very different spatial impressions by the simple expedient of changing the sizes and locations of the openings. Moving a window from the middle of a wall to a corner will utterly transform the entire character of the room.' But moving or changing the windows is a serious task, especially since planning restrictions on street elevations or farm structures often do not permit puncturing the fabric of the building. It may be impossible to lengthen or shorten windows, let alone create new ones.

The amount of daylight in former industrial or farm buildings depends largely, of course, on the windows. Barns may have small openings

1 A windowless space into which the stainless-steel galley kitchen has been fitted is illuminated by a skylight.

2 When furniture designer Nick Allen bought an old electrical warehouse in London, a windowless wall blocked out the leafy cemetery next door, so he opened up the house with modern windows. 'At least we aren't overlooked,' he jokes.

that leave the interior dim, while some industrial buildings can have floor-to-ceiling windows as high as 14m (46ft). Barns can have skylights inserted, but these have to be positioned taking into account structural features such as purlins and rafters. Others may have wind-eyes that, enlarged and glazed, will bring much-needed light indoors, or big double barn doors that might be replaced with a glazed wall.

While barns often have too little light at the core, too much light can also be a problem in some inner-city industrial buildings. The use of large sheets of transparent glass to divide space has blurred the distinction between window and wall. Clear glass in a window-wall can provide adequate daylight to a depth of about 6m (19½ft). If there are windows on the opposite walls, as in so many New York apartments, then light may penetrate indoors to a depth of 12m (39ft).

Whether you decide to filter or screen the daylight, or mask the view for the sake of privacy, depends upon several factors: the degree to which you are overlooked, the building's height above ground level, and the window area. The first thing to check as you step into the shell of an apartment is the view – a 12-storey hotel opposite, which casts shadows and blocks the morning light, will light up at night like a cruise liner. It may be that the only way adjacent dwellers can reduce light pollution – and not become reluctant voyeurs – is to live behind blinds with the lights

on all day. On the other hand, a riverfront apartment, with the water framed by the windows, reflecting the light back indoors, allows its inhabitants to live in the equivalent of an aquarium.

Wrap-around windows and the use of bright surfaces within the field of vision can cause glare. So that you do not have to wear sunglasses indoors, soften the furnishing colours, shade the windows, or tint the glass if planning permits. Matt finishes on the window frames and surrounding surfaces will help to cut the glare of reflected light. Other solutions include mechanical shading on the outside of the building, such as a canopy or an overhanging balcony. Centuries ago, ingenious solutions were devised to control the amount of daylight. Pieter de Hooch's painting *An Interior*, *with*

① To coax as much light as possible into a former warehouse, architects Paxton Locher inset a toughened glass door which opens out onto a courtyard and can pivot onto the ceiling like a garage door.

► *Clockwise from top left*: in Daniel Vial's tenth-century priory, natural light comes from small, centrally placed windows. Specially designed windows inset in brick walls are the focal point of this old coach-repair works. In a church conversion in South Africa, artist Beazy Bailey up-dated the orginal gothic windows by painting their frames an outrageous shade of cerise pink. In a 1960s factory in London, designer Ross Lovegrove and his wife Miska Miller introduced modern aluminium-framed windows to admit maximum light.

a Woman Drinking with Two Men (1658) shows a wood-panelled wall inset with a grid of small panes of glass, which is shielded two-thirds of the way up by shutters. The top windows have their wooden shutters hinged to fold flat against the raftered ceiling. The contemporary version is garage doors that slide up to lie flat against a high ceiling. These can be preferable to bi-folding shutters that require walls against which they can be folded.

Daylight changes with the time of day, time of year and weather conditions. These changes – which create marvellous patterns within an apartment – affect the way in which you orientate your living space. When planning the apartment, you should take into account the position of the windows, occupancy patterns and day-to-day tasks. Fit your own work routine and leisure time into the space available to ensure that each benefits from the best light and privacy. Interior designer Jenny Armit always sites the bed, bathing and TV-viewing areas furthest away from the windows in the belief that most people who work all day will only visit these areas when they have turned on the lights. She sites the kitchen/diner by the window for food preparation, and for weekend breakfasts when the adjacent, overlooking office building is empty.

1 The wisteria that clings to this old machine workshop in Paris creates a leafy arbour within, so the owners have dressed the windows simply.

2 In an old cement factory in Barcelona, beautiful arched windows accentuate the awesome height of the living area.

3 Interior designer Vicente Wolf lives in a former clothes manufacturing factory in New York. On three of the four sides of the building there are windows, which he prefers to leave bare. For those overlooked he uses white cotton blinds and props up pictures for privacy.

An exacting aesthetic

Minimalism to the uninitiated is the equivalent of sensory deprivation – without noise, colour, jarring interruption or weight. So the minimalist architect John Pawson was an unusual choice to renovate a beautiful eighteenth-century English barn, with its elaborate framework of purlins and braces and struts. Pawson's amazingly sympathetic trans-formation of the space has been done with an artist's touch: the backdrop of the barn is coolly distanced from his room installations, in which long, low, white screens define areas for cooking, eating and seating.

The young owners, graphic designer Sean Perkins and photographer Fi McGhee, searched every weekend for years to find an old barn to convert because they wanted farm buildings to stable their horse, with tack rooms and food-storage areas. Hidden half a mile up a track in undulating farmlands, they discovered an old Dutch hay barn surrounded by farm buildings and trees.

'What we liked best about the property was that the space

had already been simplified by function.' And yet, when the barn finally came up for sale, they knew they had to demolish large areas of it, because over the centuries interventionist rebuilding had impacted upon the simple structure of the building and complicated it.

Planning permission was granted for the demolition of one-third of the farm buildings connected to the barn, as they were not part of the original farm structure and had already partially collapsed. In addition, the entire frame of the barn had to be jacked up, the foundations rebuilt on foot plates and the oak rafters replaced after tireless sleuthing in architectural salvage yards.

The owners' admiration for the clear simplicity of space

and the integrity of traditional materials led them to architect John Pawson. Their minimal brief was 'space, light and horses', and Pawson's imaginative and uncompromising solution, is totally in keeping with the old structure and its past function. Throughout the work, he was given an entirely free hand, except in the planning of the stables for Fi's horse. The final results delighted the new owners.

Creating huge, white, empty spaces does not come cheap. Minimalism may look simple but it is an exacting aesthetic. Together with the architect came a landscape designer, heating engineer, lighting engineer, structural engineer, plumber, electrician, stonemason, craftsman and carpenter. Interference with the fabric of the old barn was kept to

'Emptiness is created for people'
JOHN PAWSON

bathtub he designed in stone (4). The furniture is suitably monastic: benches made from York stone, the geometric Donald Judd day bed (1) and a table and bed designed by John Pawson. The architect believes that 'emptiness is created for people. It is they who make space come alive. Everything is there when they need it.' Pure geometry and no upholstery is in the minimalist aesthetic. Even light switches, sockets and cables are hidden, as Pawson believes that such details spoil the uninterrupted beauty of a plain white plastered wall. Similarly, heating is always underfloor because radiators are too intrusive. Nothing spoils the simplicity of architecture, old and new.

Simplicity as a way of life means ordering and defining the everyday rituals and necessities of existence. Nothing is wasted, all is honed and pared down to its essential form; and this barn, which represents both shelter and harvest, symbolizes the honest effort John Pawson so admires.

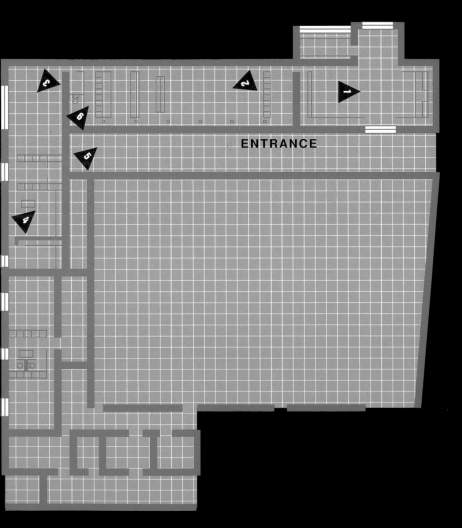

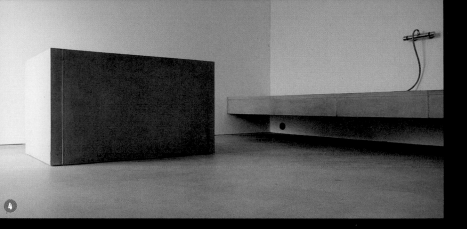

a minimum. The house was
opened up at both ends
where there were already
huge entrances for hay wains
and carts. Pawson glazed
those ends, floor to ceiling
(2, 3), then blocked off all
the windows and doors on
the other two sides of the
building. As a result, natural
light is beautifully controlled,
which is essential for Fi,
who uses the house as
her studio.

The long run, in which
carts were once left (2), now
has a dining and cooking
space at one end and a bedroom (3) with an adjoining
bath, shower and dressing
room (housing clothes and
a washing machine and
dryer) at the other. The
main barn is used as a
studio and library. Here
John Pawson designed what
is known in the household
as a 'Pawson wall' – monumental,
not reaching the top, but
serving as a screen in silkily
polished, sensuous plaster.
This supports a bench, and
is used as much to define an
area as for relaxing.

In keeping with John
Pawson's rigorous approach, practically all of the fixtures
were custom-made, from
stainless-steel worktops and
stone sinks (6) to the deep

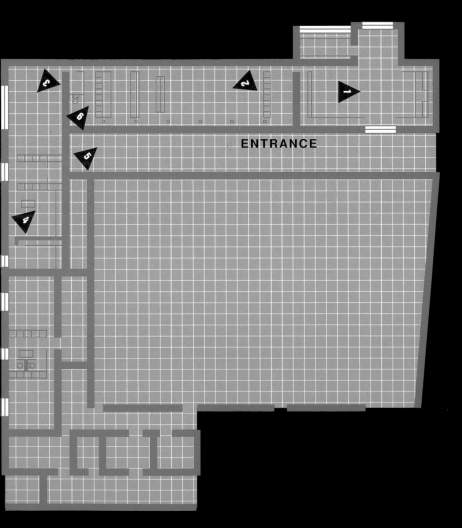

ENTRANCE

Lighting

Space can be manipulated with light. Long before the light bulb was invented, Sir John Soane used mirrored insets around windows and skylights to coax the cold northern light indoors at his studio, which is now home to a museum in London's Lincoln's Inn Fields. By night, firelight and lantern light sparkled, while mirrors and the shiny surfaces of French-polished furniture were positioned to reflect as much light as possible. You can learn from Soane's ingenuity and create different sources of light throughout a conversion to balance natural with artificial.

Contemporary architect Philip Johnson says that in his buildings light takes the form of decoration.

He uses candles in his glass house, 'a moving light, a flicker,' and by day, watching the seasons change and the lighting dim down, he calls the effect 'my wallpaper'. Depending on the amount of daylight from the windows, dormers, skylights or roof glazing, many different lighting fixtures need to be considered. General light from ceiling lights, spots, wall washers and floor lights will need backup from more focused lamps, so that light can be directed where it is needed most.

A working factory is lit by artificial light throughout the day. The sheer volume of floor space means that the core of the building is set back from the windows, the primary source of natural light.

1 Architect Andrew Berman has backlit an opalescent narrow vertical column and uses the same light source for small inset ceiling lights.

2 The vaulted ceiling in this conversion, which has been bordered with white-painted, wooden tongue-and-groove is supported by metal girders and provides an elaborate gantry for both down lighters and uplighters.

3 A change of level in this converted gymnasium in an old schoolhouse encouraged the owners to put two small spotlights into the platform floor. The curved glass creates a light core in the hall.

4 The playful banding of colour in this kitchen by Circus Architects encouraged the frivolous use of lights. Suspended on low-voltage wire, small halogen lights can be directed where needed. The system puts the fun back into functional.

5 Interior designer Jenny Armit was given the smallest and darkest show space to design in a King's Cross loft conversion in London. Into a windowless area, she put the bedroom and television-viewing area, as neither need daylight. Lighting was carefully positioned to reflect the lifestyle of a busy professional, and the bedroom was screened with curtains.

In converted apartments the furthest recesses from the façade are often windowless walls, and barns may have no windows at all. In rural conversions as well as in warehouses and factories, there is often little that can be done structurally to change the source of natural light.

Lighting consultants (usually brought in ahead of the plasterers because of the need to install power cables, controls and dimmer circuits) consider the soft furnishings and groupings of tables and chairs, sofas and chaise-longues, in order to highlight them. In big open spaces, beams of light from lamps and baffled spots on dimmer controls are needed to balance light with shade, as an evenly floodlit space can end up looking like a tennis court. Just as the quality of light varies during the course of the day, the intensity of artificial light and depth of shadow can be controlled and emphasized. In architecture, light adds a fourth dimension, highlighting walls or reducing their volume. Wall surfaces painted white, or in a colour, will change the effect of a space when bathed in light. The quality of light also changes according to the reflective nature of a background.

There are two approaches to artificial light: the architectural approach, for which fixtures are built into the fabric of the buildings, and the decorative approach, involving lamps and shades. Lights can be mounted on the walls as uplighters, or reversed, higher up, to become downlighters. They can be recessed discreetly into the floors like miniature light boxes to cast light upwards, or set in ceilings as low-voltage fixtures.

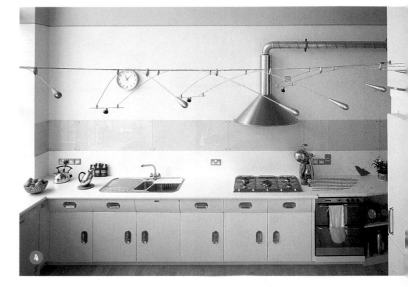

The decorative approach relies on wall sconces and different lamps placed around the room. Table lamps require tables dotted evenly about the space and long extension cords that have to be concealed underneath rugs so there are no bundles of wiring visible. Freestanding lamps

of halogen light should be avoided, since it fights with the architectural framework.

There are different qualities of light. Fluorescent light is unforgiving and tends to be whiter than halogen or metal halide, but a new generation of compact fluorescents are long-lasting and can be useful for ceiling, wall or floor lights. Diffusing light behind shades or baffles will create a warmer, softer effect. Aluminium lighting cornices are a useful way of introducing detailing to a room as they emit two-directional light from shades. Decorators tend to avoid overhead lighting because it can be unflattering, but in high-ceilinged rooms architects often use it because a shadowy, vaulted ceiling can be gloomy.

If the arrangement of space is the first decision in a loft conversion, then the choice of lighting has to be second. Decorator Charles Rutherfoord's table lamps may look wonderful in a traditional drawing room, but in a big, open-plan living space they can appear dinky. They also look deadly when switched off during the day – 'rows of dull shades on tables'. Rutherfoord believes peppering the ceiling with a starburst

1 Architects Wells Macreth put floor lighting set in slate in the shower area, and downlighters in the ceiling behind glass-fronted closets.

2 In his London loft, architect Martin Lee uses pendant 'Titania' suspension lights made by Luceplan, which have coloured filters that can be inset into the delicate skeletal frame.

3 Floor lights behind blinds that roll up from the floor give extra light at small windows.

4 Lighting designer André Tammes uses floor lighting to make a feature of rough wooden columns, and contrasts a central Shaker-style candelabra with small, pendant low-voltage lights in the dining area.

5 For maximum light in this New York loft, architects Hanrahan Meyers combined partially opaque light blocks with halogen downlighters.

contain a photographic filter that softens the light and gives it the colour-quality of a tungsten lamp.

Clip-on picture lights and wall sconces reinforce light for reading. Mid-height fixtures, either mounted on the wall or freestanding, bring light down to a human level and make a room feel more cosy. In open-plan living areas dimmer switches are essential. Interior designer Lady Victoria Waymouth believes that 'a successful dinner party means at least three levels of light on dimmer': perhaps a chandelier at high level, lamps or concealed lighting in a bookcase or wall surround and candles on the sideboard. The important thing to remember is that the fixtures should be as discreet as possible. Ideally, the source – the light bulb – should not be visible. In the open environment of the industrial space, many different light sources can be mixed with pyrotechnic skill to create a sense of excitement.

3 Walls

The Architectural Shell

In factories or warehouses, where there are never any conventional internal support walls, there is opportunity for more shapely, free-form space dividers. Architect Frank Lloyd Wright heralded this new freedom to do away with permanent floor-to-ceiling walls when he wrote that 'Americans, seeking culture, could not accept that posts and beams could be thrown away in favor of folding or moveable planes, nor that organic architecture could derive from the tall grass of the mid-western prairies.' Curved glass-block walls, fibreboard partitions, curled, spiralled and freestanding walls, and steel shower cubicles are more interesting options for dividing space than bricks and mortar.

A modern translation of Frank Lloyd Wright's idea snakes sinuously along the length of a

windowless warehouse conversion that is home to London-based architects Jan Kaplicky and Amanda Levete of Future Systems. From the front door (the only door in the open-plan apartment), a partition screen planted some distance from the shared wall curls around to provide a bathing cubicle, stretches out to become the splashback for kitchen work-tops and then spirals into a round bed. Made from medium density fibreboard (MDF) and spray-gunned with car paint in shocking pink, lime and purple, it doubles as both architectonic furniture and interior wall. Standing only two-thirds of the floor-to-ceiling height, it does not block out the light in a

windowless ground floor that is lit by day from an overhead skylight. To help the flow of natural light, choose partitions made of paper, either the age-old Japanese *shoji* rice-paper screens, framed in balsa wood to make robust sliding panels, or those made of a paper by DuPont called Tryvek, which is tough enough to withstand bumps, soaking and freezing, and can be wiped clean.

More substantial than paper partitions are the new versatile glass panels that also diffuse light. Glass can now be coated with mole-cules to create photochromic glass that reacts to ultraviolet light and darkens as the light increases. Or, as with electrochromic glass,

The new generation of glass is capable of changing in response to light and electrical impulses. Photochromic glass is coated with molecules that change according to daylight levels, and electrochromic glass changes from clear to opaque on an electrical current.

1 Twenty square panes of glass create a light wall for the combined living area and workspace in a conversion by Gilles Bouchez. The central panel pivots, opening into the courtyard, and the panes on the upper floor allow the maximum amount of daylight to penetrate into the core of the building.

2 For a show space in London's Saffron Hill, Nick Hockley at architects ORMS has installed an opaque glass wall.

3 A vast, pivoting panelled door made of toughened glass is replicated by a glass panel suspended from the ceiling to admit light from the windows above.

flip from clear to opaque when an electrical impulse triggers the change. Eventually, whole buildings will be made of this responsive glass, but for the moment the technology is only affordable on a relatively small scale, and is mainly found in innovative loft conversions.

Mark Guard, who created an electrochromic glass shower, has devised a number of surprising walls, including sliding walls that open to reveal beds folded flat, centrally hinged pivotal panels that part to reveal kitchens, or showers in niches. He has also created a spring-loaded panel that opens into a study area in a master bedroom.

1 At the furthest recesses of his Cape Town apartment in an old warehouse, Craig Port installed a shower partially shielded by a glass-brick wall that forms the backdrop to an old ceramic sink.

2 Architect Nico Rensch took his inspiration from the East in using plywood and Japanese paper sliding panels to filter natural daylight.

3 In a New York loft a customized floor-to-ceiling door is cut to a template to fit into the sliding partition wall. Rather than interrupt the flow of light, a second wall between the living room and study is made from big square panes of glass set within narrow glazing bars.

4 In this converted cinema in Fife, Scotland, the white bed is separated from the dark antiques by a diaphanous full-length white gauzy curtain. The curtain rolls to the far end of the open space where the newly inserted window wall has a view to the sea.

Glass bricks are ideal for dividing rooms with different light requirements. The way light passes through glass bricks varies according to the type of brick used. There are fully transparent bricks, frosted ones that refract light, or satin-finished glass that lets in light while remaining opaque. In a redbrick Victorian warehouse conversion, where the view across the river has been opened up with window-walls, the architect decided on only one interior wall: a frosted-glass block wall that separates the shower from the bed deck. These sculptural glass walls cannot be used for shelving or to hang pictures, which is why, in most cases, they are sited either around bathing cubicles or at entrances where fire regulations specify double doors.

One of the considerations of a large glass span is the amount of cold (and heat) that will be transferred from windows or interior window-walls. Nonagenarian Philip Johnson, one of America's greatest architects, confesses that his famously modern all-glass

1 Above the old skirting board (baseboard) in a former Oddfellows Lodge belonging to Robert Indiana, the dado rail and decorative border can still be seen, providing the inspiration for a boldly patterned wall-to-wall carpet. Indiana's own dramatic painting propped up on a fabric-covered chest creates a focal point in the room.

2 In a schoolhouse built in 1929, the owner set the blackboards, framed in mahogany with chalk runners, against white-plastered walls, and furnished the room with functional simplicity.

3 This American conversion was given a rustic look by leaving the wooden walls unclad and rubbing in a pale grey to resemble driftwood.

4 It was important to make external openings in a dairy as small as possible to keep the space cool and dimly lit. In this conversion in Toronto, the original windows, placed high to exclude sunlight, were retained. White plaster walls and floor are the perfect background for a simple arrangement of furniture.

Existing walls are seldom good-looking, and are often in the wrong place once the factory floor has been carved up into apartments. Interior designers sometimes work around these walls to diminish their bulk. Architect Eva Jiřičná styled a protruding chimney breast into the form of a ziggurat in a London apartment which no longer had a hearth. Alternatively, the wall can be given a supporting role in the new scheme, becoming a showcase for pictures, a backdrop to a library, a support for folding beds, or having metal stair treads bracketed to it. As they gain purpose, walls seem less of an obstruction.

Adding new finishes to existing walls and beams, or revealing more attractive old finishes, also makes them easier to live with. Bare brick or smoke-grey cement can be tamed in the way furniture designer James Hong did in his converted top-floor warehouse in New York. By rubbing coloured pigments into wet concrete and applying it with a trowel to bath panels, he achieved the unimaginable – he made cement look chic. Sometimes surprises await the DIY enthusiast: removing the industrial grime in a former millinery factory in Melbourne, Australian photographer Mark Chew and his wife Sally Ann Ballharrie scraped down beams that looked like steel girders but turned out to be Oregon pine.

In the same way, video-maker Zanna discovered the Arts and Crafts origins of her converted schoolhouse in the peeling wallpaper. By ripping the layers a little more she was able to expose the different designs of the decades. This archival collage of applied arts in her 'adult kindergarten', as she calls the schoolhouse, will puzzle archaeologists of the future.

Large expanses of window-walls actually leave less space for display. Andrée Putman had to reduce the number of works of art she had collected when she moved into her bigger apartment in Paris. Harry Handelsman, chairman of the

1 Wooden lathe walls without plaster are an unusual touch in an industrial space.

▶ *Clockwise from top left*: a smoothly plastered curved wall is an unexpected feature in an old barn on the Norfolk coast. A ladder radiator silhouetted behind an opaque glass wall makes a geometric pattern with the walls and stairs. A barn is given a modern industrial finish with a corrugated plastic internal wall, and rafters and support clad in brushed stainless steel. Canvas rigged tightly on a steel frame creates a shield for a shower, which has been positioned near the kitchen to utilise the water source and service points. The walls in this Wells Fargo warehouse, Jersey City, are 15m (49ft) high, permitting a giddying mix of wall coverings and styles. Glass panels above a wooden partition create an opalescent backdrop to carefully hung pictures.

Manhattan Loft Co., discovered within his own penthouse conversion at Bankside, London, that the curved walls left him insufficient space to hang his burgeoning art collection. Yet many people envisage a loft space as the ideal background for their art collection. German-born architect Annabelle Selldorf says that she is often asked to remodel New York lofts for art collectors because she interprets the dwelling space in the same way as a gallery, asking: Where do you have a good wall? How are you going to hang art there? How are you going to make this room a good viewing space? By her definition, a 'good wall' is one that has been made monumental or thinned down to compensate for poor room

1 Piers Gough at architects CZWG specified leather for the walls of this elegant conversion for the Manhattan Loft Co. in London. Soft cowhide stretched taut beneath the vaulted ceiling and edged with a wooden skirting board (baseboard) weathers well with time.

2 Film-set designer Richard Ferbrache lined the walls of his factory conversion in Toronto with bank-deposit boxes, arranging them to make the most of their brass hinges and key-holes. The doorway, which is designed to look like a hole blown in the wall, was inspired by the wall covering.

proportions. In a loft conversion in New York she described the original dining room as 'a long, skinny space separated from the living room by a wall that was way too thin'. The openings were 'oddly sized and misplaced'. The ungainly length of that living area was improved simply by thickening the wall to the depth of a chunky armoire, while the long, narrow dining space was halved to create a study behind a slender wall of backlit bi-folding glass doors.

Whether monumental or significantly slender, walls play a major part in altering a space. Interior design can minimize their visual impact, but they must always be considered at the initial planning stage, to meet the need for privacy and light (both natural and artificial). Employ a structural engineer if walls are to be removed.

Floors

The reinforced load-bearing ceilings in one apartment become the solid concrete floors in the apartment above. Buildings designed to support heavy equipment have reinforced joists on every floor to help bear exceptional loads. The advantage of this is that they will support anything from a whirlpool bath to a heavyweight antique four-poster bed, or even a roof garden (not all roofs are load bearing, so this must be checked). The disadvantage is that floor levels within these solid structures are difficult to change. Even siting a sunken bath can be as compli-cated as sinking an oil well.

Changing the floor surface over such a large area has a huge impact on the space, but it can also be expensive, which is why many loft dwellers look for interesting hard-surface composites. For the floors in

Milan's smartest contemporary furniture store, Cappellini, British industrial designer Jasper Morrison mixed resin into concrete and poured it over the floor. The burnished, silken, silvery-grey finish looks more like stone than cement but costs a third of the price. Composites – largely the product of an imaginative mind – give a more textured finish; coloured quartz pebbles set in resin can be bought ready-mixed for use on concrete floors. Peter Elliott laid a new kitchen floor with river pebbles set in concrete, which he then had polished smooth with a terrazzo grinder. The rest of his Melbourne warehouse apartment had limed (pickled) Tasmanian hardwood floors that he could not hope to replicate. So instead he changed direction, demarcating specific areas with different flooring effects.

Heavy-duty flooring in some industrial buildings can be difficult to incorporate into every-day living. Deep trenches once housed cables in the polished concrete floor of a former power plant in Texas. Converting it into a home, architect Gary Cunningham used these trenches for the domes-tic electricity cables and then covered them with triple-laminate armoured glass, through which they can still be seen. Walking on glass can be an intimidating prospect, but special toughened

There is no quicker way to focus attention on any particular part of a living space than to cover it with pattern. Pattern is often introduced or altered so as to direct people visually to a change in the function of an area.

1 Pebbles of similar sizes and shades, collected from the seashore and raked over the floor of a twelfth-century farm building in Majorca, have been embedded in cement.

2 The Cubist-inspired painting on this linoleum floor has been protected with a sealant.

3 In a converted drinks factory in Brooklyn, Paul Ochs and the late Argentinian painter Osvaldo Gomariz retained the original stone slab floor and separated the living space from the studio by a raised wooden platform.

glass can support tremendous weights, even acting as the surround for an indoor swimming pool. Due to the need to diffuse light – often from skylights – through vast volumes of space, some architects favour the use of glass at junctions like stair landings. Rick Mather specified glass walkways and stair landings in a bachelor apartment so that light could filter into the entrance hall below.

The big investment for many home-owners is a wooden floor. Older industrial buildings, particularly those situated on waterfronts and used for the unloading of raw materials and foodstuffs, may have wooden floors of broad, mellowed

boards. Many home-owners prefer to reclaim old wooden floors from former gymnasiums or schools because the solid oak or beech boards are so much broader than contemporary veneers. However, finding recycled floorboards from salvage companies and having them laid requires patient detective work and an expert carpenter. Industrial designer Ross Lovegrove and his architect wife, Miska Miller, kept the floorboards in their warehouse conversion in London even though they were marked and studded with nail holes. All the original nail holes have now been filled in with studs of car-body filler in fluorescent colours.

Wood veneers, rubber, linoleum and even cement coloured with pigment and burnished smooth are some of the less expensive options for big areas. Wood veneers have to be laid in traditional block patterns, onto planks which slot

closely together, so that when they are in place you can scarcely see the joins. Alternative floor surfaces can distinguish a functional area, for example beaten stainless-steel panels for heavy-duty areas like kitchens or entrances. Linoleum has recently come out of the landlady's closet to feature as one of the most versatile materials in contemporary design. In the conversion of Philip and Carol Thomas's banking hall, the traditional checked linoleum floor has made a comeback, as the owners found it a more affordable alternative to travertine marble.

Changing the floor covering gives the occupant the chance to change levels, maybe step down into a living area or up to the dining area. Not all these changes in levels are fanciful – sometimes they are essential. When three Victorian classrooms in London, each occupying an entire floor measuring

1 The skill in planning a conversion lies in making the most of what can be salvaged. Here Suzanne Lumsden kept the broad wooden boards of the original church floor.

2 Three types of floor covering indicate three different areas: the small matt grey mosaic tiles of the entrance hall change to a wooden floor in the dining area, which in turn gives way to pale wall-to-wall carpet for the living space in architect Vincent van Duysen's Antwerp apartment.

3 Instead of embarking on the painstaking detective work involved in sourcing recycled floorboards from salvage companies, the owners of this space decided on a practical plywood floor.

24m (80ft) long by 7m (23ft) wide, beneath 4m (14ft)-high ceilings, were converted into a family house for Julian Metcalfe, founder of the fast-food chain Prêt à Manger, the floors were raised on the ground floor. Windows had been placed high up – to prevent children from staring out – and planning permission would not permit changing them. The first thing designer Willie Nickerson did was to raise the floor by 50cm (1^1/$_2$ft) to make more use of these evenly placed windows, which now bathe the seated inhabitants in natural light, thereby changing the proportions of the space for the better. Dividing the Sahara-sized expanse of the kitchen, dining and living area with partitions would have turned the attic into a dolls' house, so instead Nickerson used floor furnishings to create conversation areas. Oases of calm, dotted about with kilims and needlepoint rugs, around which he set comfortable club chairs, some modern furniture and bookcases, gave the open space what the designer describes as a 'bookish feeling'. This solution not only divides the space, it also cuts the echo with soft furnishings.

1 In a converted wood-polish factory, interior designer Michael Green painted the floorboards with white gloss and then sealed them with several coats of varnish before laying a separate section of square white ceramic tiles.

2 A metal-grille walkway with halyard rigging for the banisters prevents the light from being blocked in this apartment.

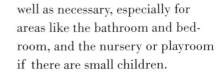

Split Levels & Stairs

The Architectural Shell

Most inner-city dwellings are vertical, so the space tends to be tall and narrow. It is unusual to find a horizontal space opening out on the lines of a Miesian pavilion or a Frank Lloyd Wright prairie house. Within an industrial or agricultural building the space is usually expansive and open, and there are no basements, landings or attics. However, some division of space is often desirable as well as necessary, especially for areas like the bathroom and bedroom, and the nursery or playroom if there are small children.

Living on different levels is an obvious way to inhabit these voluminous apartments without blocking the view or the flow of light with partitioning. A mezzanine pitched against a windowless back wall – to avoid breaking up a floor-to-ceiling glazed frontage – becomes a sleeping, dining or study area that does not depend upon a great deal of natural light.

Split-level living can be as simple as a platform bed built from scaffolding or as complicated as a network of interconnecting walkways like the film set for *Alien*, with capsules off it for

Rather than break up an area with solid walls, many conversions have been designed to allow space to flow freely. Here, architects have added mezzanine floors reached by ladders, stairs or walkways.

1 A ladder leads to a rooftop eyrie created by slinging a hammock between roof beams. Since it is at a vertiginous height, it is protected by a thick beam.

2 An enormouse loft space in New York, designed by architects Kiss Cathcart Anders permits *Indiana Jones*-style walkways. Ladders lead to a mezzanine floor beneath the aircraft-hangar-like ceiling.

sleeping or bathing. Within a lofty apartment in London with wrap-around industrial windows on two sides and bare brick walls on the other two, photographer Bob Baldwin set a platform on top of stilts to create a sleeping space that has some of the pioneering spirit of its owner. Salvaged lumber and hand-hewn beams combined with old brick walls show a simplicity and spontaneity.

Because they are high ceilinged, farm buildings also lend themselves to split-level living. In

① Reinforced-steel joists support a platform or mezzanine floor. The volume of space between floor and ceiling in this apartment permits a kitchen on the landing, with stairs to dining areas both above and below. Consider the view from beneath a mezzanine: steel joists painted black make contemporary rafters.

② This inner-city apartment has such high ceilings that the owners were able to paint them strong yellow and bring the colour down onto the pillars between the windows, a scheme that has influenced the furnishing of their galleried living space.

John Stephanidis's oak-timbered dairy, ground-floor stalls have been converted into living spaces.

Bedrooms in barns can be built into the eaves under high-pitched, A-frame roofs where sheaves of grain were once thrashed. Ladders that once enabled farmhands to descend from the haymows are used by young family members to reach their double bunk beds.

Factories and warehouses tend to have reinforced, load-bearing floors, so deep bathtubs and even swimming pools can be sited on an upper floor. Architects Heidi Locher and Richard Paxton took advantage of the sturdy concrete floors within their former printing works to build

an indoor swimming pool up-stairs. They could swim, work, cook, entertain and watch television, all without leaving the mezzanine floor.

In a daring sleight of hand, architect Seth Stein removed the partition walls in a converted London penthouse built a century ago by Sir Edwin Lutyens. Within the 19m (62ft)-long, 6m (20ft)-high open-plan living space, a 3m (10ft)-high mezzanine gallery provides room for a study at one end and the owners' gym at the other. Instead of a traditional bathroom beneath these high ceilings, a 4m (12ft)-high cylindrical tower houses a whirlpool bath at its top level, and a shower cubicle below.

volume. A favourite lightweight – but strong – material for stair treads is industrial steel mesh with diamond-mesh iron risers. Light filters through the perforations, making them almost transparent.

Stairs can be as simple as the ladders used to reach bunk beds in a converted hayloft or as complex as staircases with metal treads and yachting halyards for banisters. They can lead to glazed rooftop kitchens in the sky, sleeping places under the stars, or down to whirlpool baths or hot tubs. But even if a staircase only constitutes a short run to a mezzanine floor it will not be unobtrusive. Designed to carry a lot of traffic, the staircase will need to be carefully tailored.

Door handles used to be the architectural equivalent of worry beads, but since there are so few doors in industrial conversions, the new designer enthusiasm is for staircases. Structural simplicity is the great goal. As the architectural historian Nikolaus Pevsner succinctly put it, 'In twentieth-century architecture the staircase assumes a new significance as the element in a building which is most expressive of spatial flow.'

Staircases take up a lot of room. Even a spiral staircase requires at least 2sq.m (21½sq.ft) to allow for comfortable treads. In some conversions the existing stairs are worth preserving and highlighting: many industrial buildings retain the cast-iron staircases used as fire escapes. In an old forge, architect Tim Wood and his wife Carol went further than preservation to let the original spiral staircase determine the layout of their open-plan living area. Only their bedroom and bathroom are behind closed doors and they have sited their bath on a raised platform at the foot of the staircase.

New staircases, on the other hand, need to look weightless and poised, a difficult task given the height and

1 A simple change in level from the concrete entrance hall is delineated by a solid wooden block – a seating platform at ground level. From this a zigzagging wooden stair ascends to the platform above.

▶ Sometimes stairs must be fitted into a minimal space and make a tight return. In other places they can extend their tread to become the focal point of the space. *Clockwise from top left*: a spiralling steel staircase makes the most of an inner core illuminated by a porthole window. Stone slabs leading in three directions form a simple staircase in a converted farm building. Elaborate cast-iron stairs double back on themselves from a small steel landing. A pair of steel staircases flank a vaulted window.

Services

It is the things you cannot see because they are usually hidden by cladding – plumbing, electricity, ducting – that consume the most time and money in a conversion. Pipes that carried large volumes of water and waste, as well as ducting that held the bundles of cables suitable for servicing a factory, may be more obtrusive than the new occupants desire. Today's lofts are gentrified; false ceilings and floors take advantage of the soaring vertical spaces to hide many essential services. But there are also those who prefer the services exposed.

All buildings are subject to their own constraints, particularly with regard to the location of drainage. Sewer drainage points can be awkward because waste only travels one way – downwards; electricity, water and gas supplies can travel around doors and up or down walls, but plumbing cannot. Architect Piers Gough advises any purchaser of an

industrial shell to check that there are drainage outlets on either side of the entrance to allow kitchens, cloakrooms and bathrooms to be sited anywhere within the space.

In Finland, vacuum-suction waste systems have been developed that operate much like airline washroom facilities to break this dependence on plumbing. But it is easier and less expensive to operate within the existing drainage system. Dismissing the notion of the new vacuum water closets, Piers Gough warns, 'Someone will put their tights down them and that's the end of them. All systems go wrong, and that is the major thing to remember.' There is a simple rule to installing the latest technology, he believes: 'Ask yourself if you can work your

video and if you can't, do not
install complicated equipment
to run your house.'

Interior designer Jenny Armit has
learned to work around the basic
services. In a former telephone
exchange, a gigantic crossbar, which
once fed the ducting system and
cabling, dissected the ceiling. The
developer resisted all arguments to
have the beam removed, so Armit
wired a twirly blue extendable cable
into its sturdy, cable-bearing form
and linked it to a silvered unit
that houses the oven and cooking
surfaces. The workstation can be
moved easily around the kitchen –
next to the sink, or facing away
from the dining area to act as a
screen. So, a major structural defect
has become an amusing adaptation
for a mobile workstation.

Investigations into cavernous
spaces often produce unpleasant
surprises. Combining two 165sq.m

1 Tongue-and-groove boards reach two-thirds
of the way up the wall to create a room installation for a shower cubicle. The original pipes
and sprinkler system of this old warehouse in
TriBeCa, overlooking the Hudson River, illustrate
how the old can meet the new.

2 In an old power station in Dallas, architect
Gary Cunningham glazed over the deep power-
cable channels in the cement floor. Furniture on
castors moves smoothly across these divisions.

3 New ventilation ducts are part of the wood-
and-metal scheme in this loft, blending with the
upper walkways and mezzanine floors.

(1,800sq.ft) apartments in lower
Manhattan into one huge space,
architect Matthew Bialecki
discovered a vast concrete
support wall between them.
Added to this, a number of
pipes and ducts collided across
the wall. Undeterred, he looked
upon the tangle of equipment
as 'a country with boulders and
trees' and set about 'landscaping'
it behind pearwood panelling.
Plaster wall surfaces and a
backlit, curved Murano glass
ceiling over the brushed-pewter-
panelled kitchen all distract attention and diminish its prominence.

Heating these vast spaces can
be a problem, but one that can
be resolved by hunting around
salvage yards. Huge radiators
used in former hospitals or schools
were not designed on a domestic
scale and so suit industrial conversions. Elongated towel rails, ladder
radiators, and classic concertina-
barred or gilled radiators in
enamelled steel are all handsome
pieces. In an open-plan garage
conversion, a Cactus radiator –
designed by Paul Priestman and
named to reflect its unusual shape
– stands aloof against 14m (46ft)
of honeyed brick wall.

Underfloor heating systems,
as their name suggests, can be
concealed beneath the floor to
warm the entire surface area.
They run at surprisingly low
temperatures, which allows the

use of a wide range of flooring finishes. However, raised wooden floors that conceal underfloor heating pipes need to be installed by an expert carpenter, as wood will expand and contract, which may leave gaps between the floorboards.

Old farm buildings, where crops were dried so that they did not rot or mildew, inspire unusual heating and cooling solutions from contemporary architects who have to restrict CFC emissions – air conditioning being the worst offender. Flue-cured tobacco barns or oast houses, where hops are dried before joining the brewing process, are good examples of the principle that hot air rises. Vents at the base allow cool air in, while the tilted towers drag the warmed air up and away. In converting a magistrates' court in Bordeaux from an old oast house Richard Rogers adapted the tilted roof line to provide an efficient heating system for seven courtrooms. Cool pipes draw up a natural flow of air and disperse it, while vents in the system drive the hot air downwards in winter to heat the building.

When considering artificial lighting, remember that all lamps can be set in a small ring of 3 amps on a separate lighting circuit so that they can be switched off easily from a bank of switches by a door, rather than having

1 Salvage yards are a good source of heating on the right industrial scale. An old radiator from a hospital, still in its original state, becomes a talking point in this sleekly modern conversion.

2 In their conversion of an old garage, industrial designer Paul Priestman and his graphic-designer wife Tessa heated their open-plan living space with the sculptural Cactus radiator, prickling with heat, that Paul designed for Bisque. It forms an elegant background to a chaise-longue by Le Corbusier and the Formula One racing tyre that Paul turned into a footstool.

to be turned off separately. It may seem a small point, but in big open spaces with a lot of lights, there is something medieval about lighting each lamp individually. Wires can be passed under the floor and fed into sockets on the floor surface, or set in the more complicated floor-boxes that usually house telephone points (sockets), aerials and plugs.

Sound systems also need to be considered when wiring an open-plan living space. Having more than one pair of loudspeakers immediately allows greater sound control, but the simplest means of overall control of a sound system is via volume controls sited on the walls. Other hi-tech options involve infra-red sensors, keypads and touch screens.

The common areas in an urban loft conversion should always be thoroughly investigated, since they can be the cause of a breakdown in good neighbourliness.

Some countries legislate to govern the disposal of waste, and some lofts have organized recycling points with bottle banks, newspaper collection and waste-disposal systems in common areas. (Rural conversions may not have these communal facilities.) Due to the difficulty in arranging these services to suit individual needs, many developers provide an in-house designer who offers a 'fit and build' service for the whole building. In the initial stages of design and configuration, the designer will take each owner through the building-control regulations and allow you to tap into these central services.

Fruit Factory, Antwerp

The power of colour

Trucks used to pull up inside this 1960s fruit juice factory to unload their contents into three gigantic silos. Maybe it was their colourful cargo that inspired the new owners to grow a banana tree indoors and display it against watermelon, orange and lemon walls. Maybe it was the soft grey showery light of Belgium that suggested the intense palette with vibrant colour accents, as much as the seamless way in which outdoors becomes indoors. Terraces front and back, a winter sitting room and a summer salon make this a house for all seasons.

When Kathleen Van Zandweghe and Joris Mampaey discovered the 1,000sq.m (10,760sq.ft) fruit juice factory 14.5km (about 9 miles) outside Antwerp, it was derelict. An insulation manufacturer had taken over the factory and then moved on, leaving behind vermiculite, other raw materials and formidable amounts of rubbish. The flat roof leaked, all the windows were broken, the grass was thigh-high. But Kathleen could see the beauty and, importantly, 'the correct proportions of the whole construction'. The first principle driving their conversion was the need to maintain the proportions of the original space. Kathleen had the ideas and Joris drew them up.

But before they made structural changes, they considered the orientation of the building. The factory's street elevation faces east. There is a neighbouring house to one side and a paddock on the other. The west-facing back of the building overlooks farmland and woods. This position determined the owners' early decision to widen some of the windows to enhance natural light, and block off others to increase privacy, as well as adding two terraces to the building.

There were no planning restrictions limiting them, but the couple's determination not to interfere with the proportions of the building meant that they kept the original windows on the façade. A symmetrical pair of vast rectangular windows on the street façade, each measuring 5 × 3.5m (16 × 11ft), was framed with iron bars made by a blacksmith, to keep the profile as streamlined as possible. Kathleen and Joris moved the main entrance from the street elevation to the southeast-facing side of the house in a well below ground level. A few high, north-facing windows that let a harsh, cold grey light into their winter living room were blocked off, but French doors that open out onto the back garden are new. Because the main living, sleeping and bathing spaces are 1m (3.2ft) above street level, they are not visible to passers-by, except on one side, where the owners put sand-blasted glass panes in the lower half

of the windows. All wall lights – both uplighters and downlighters – are installed at a uniform height of 1.6m (5ft). In addition, floor and table lamps, some with colourful Murano glass shades, dot light where it is needed at a more human scale.

When the fruit factory was just an architectural shell, the couple moved into one room to work out how they wanted to inhabit the space. They configured living and eating spaces across the northern front of the house, with bathrooms adjoining the sleeping space at the back in the southern half. Trees filter the daylight and there are no curtains or blinds. 'This space-planning came about as naturally as female intuition,' says Kathleen.

'Colours are simply our watermark'
KATHLEEN VAN ZANDWEGHE AND JORIS MAMPAEY

3

They sited the winter sitting room in the former storeroom (5–7, 9) and installed a big glass partition to transmit light between it and the next room, which formerly housed the heavy equipment. This cavernous space now acts as their summer salon. Here the floor had to be raised, since it originally lay 1.6m (5ft) below garden level. In summer the couple spend a lot of time on the terrace (1), which seamlessly flows into the summer salon. With a climate they describe as 'bright with showers', they are 'able to enjoy the back terrace, but quickly flee inside when it's pouring'. Before putting in new floors, they laid pipes for gas-fired central heating throughout. There are three fireplaces in the main living areas, all framed with steel. One, installed in a wall in the winter sitting room, was inspired by the architect Mallet-Stevens.

In this way, a room built to house a huge engine became habitable. Even two silos for fruit storage, somewhat modified, have a functional role in the conversion. One houses a staircase to the summer salon, and the other the kitchen (2). Connected by walkways to the sleeping area (8), winter sitting room, front room and bathroom, the kitchen workstation is seen as a hub, accessed by various pods. To ensure a positive response to the enquiry 'What's the weather like up there?' a radiant hot-water heating panel was installed.

With such vast surfaces to cover, Kathleen and Joris decided to not introduce too many changes of texture, except underfoot. By plastering the walls and keeping the stairs in concrete, they introduced a blank canvas which they subsequently painted in dazzling colours. Floors sparkle and delight with changes of pattern and material. More than ten thousand little polished-steel rectangles are glued onto the cement floor of the bedroom, forming the dramatic, matt-black background for Le Corbusier leather chairs. Glass mosaics made with a mix of tiny, smoky grey-blue tiles define the bathroom floor, while orange linoleum in the winter sitting room is waxed to a caramel glaze. In the summer salon, where exposed-brick walls have been

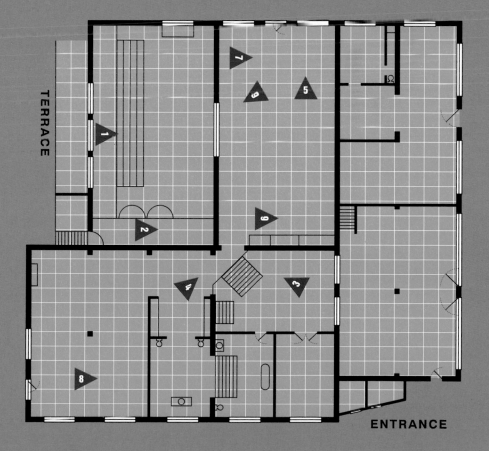

plastered just a third of the way up and then painted an ultramarine blue, the concrete floor is covered by varnished wooden boards, striped at regular intervals with broken lines. Resembling simplified road markings, the stripes are painted in red and white.

Kathleen has proved it is possible to use paint effects, upholstery and colour – all decorator's tricks – within an industrial space, without taming it too much. That boldness relies largely upon her painterly skills and adventurous spirit. Nothing too slick, rather a more vigorous, hands-on spontaneity. To disguise a door in the winter sitting room, she painted a diagonal stripe across it with the aid of masking tape, and then painted over this lightly to get rid of the rigid straight lines. When she does introduce big planes of a strong orange or pink or blue, she uses accent colours like an abstract painter. Only in the bathroom did she keep to a monochrome scheme, but even here the floor mosaic inspired by constructivist paintings is built up using different tones of the same colour, from white to grey to charcoal. In the lower level, the bath, encased in rough concrete, is backed by a wall featuring a play on perspectives, made with flat areas of white, grey and black. But then, the couple admit that 'colours are simply our watermark'. The industrial roots of the building have inspired a rougher, tougher approach to the applied arts.

The conversion of forlorn old buildings into fashionable homes defies conventional home-making to
awaken the pioneering spirit in their occupants. People
who set up home in a bottling plant or ice-storage
factory are prepared to take risks to achieve a home
that has plenty of natural light and space. Seamless
walls, sandblasted brickwork, exposed pipes, concrete
ceilings and riveted ironwork do not faze them. The
movement that started with artists in New York and
Paris needing workspace for their oversized canvases
has become the ultimate in urban chic around the
world as it allows people to buy a lifestyle along with
an empty shell. The conversions are adventurous and
on the cutting edge of design. No longer do real-
estate agents viewing the property ask the long-term
owners of a sparsely furnished conversion if they have
just moved in. This is the new and stylish way to live,
and if it comes with an attitude, so much the better.

But as Ralph Ardill, director of the Imagination
Gallery in London, warns after making his own loft
space functional – an exercise that cost him twice the
time and money he expected – 'If you are doing it as
a fashion statement, don't bother, buy a Porsche.'
Allocating space for sleeping, eating and cooking,
working, bathing, entertaining friends or just loung-
ing around can be an exacting task when you have no
rooms. The size of the space alone is often daunting.
A double-height loft in a converted industrial building
can be on an heroic scale, with roughly the floor space
of a three-bedroomed house. In the United States
people would laugh if you called something under
93sq.m (1,000sq.ft) a loft. You can play football, do
cartwheels or ride bikes in your open-plan residence,
but your furniture may drift in a sea of space without
partition walls dividing that open space into rooms.

1 Interior walls and a lowered ceiling give a strong horizontal line and
a human scale to this lofty converted church.

2 Stainless-steel appliances in a barn conversion emphasize its
modern-day function without changing its vernacular style.

For that reason, you will probably want to create a
floor plan, making certain areas suit particular needs.
Natural light often determines the positioning of the
areas in which you will spend most of your time, and
bathing and sleeping areas tend to be zoned in the
dimmest recesses. But if you are at home only at night
and watch a lot of television or surf the Internet, position your television or computer away from daylight
sources. Or if you prefer an intimate dining area rather
than one with a view, set up a table in the inner core,
or against a windowless wall. Furniture helps denote
the function of areas: chunky sofas pull up around
the television, working walls of cupboards divide
sleeping areas, freestanding kitchen equipment acts as
partitioning, a wall of glass blocks encircles a bathing
area or hides unsightly regulation fire doors from view.

Flexibility is what is on offer. Some people miss
the point of loft conversions and immediately put
in walls to make three bedrooms and two bathrooms
when they could decide to have a kitchen three times
the size of anyone else's living room or a bathroom
that doubles as a study. Each area can be as elaborate
or as simple as your lifestyle dictates – a kitchen out-
fitted to accommodate a chef, or a cubicle with an
espresso machine and a microwave. In an industrial
conversion, habits inform the habitat.

4 Entrances

In place of the sisal doormat that says 'Welcome', the visitor to a converted, fortressed factory is more likely to be greeted by a barking microchip on the entry-phone system. If the computerized modern building in Philip Kerr's thriller *GridIron* becomes a reality, every foyer will have a video hologram greeter speaking like Alec Guinness.

Factories needed large entrances to accommodate a surge of employees, so communal entrance lobbies or foyers in these buildings are usually on a grand scale. The central space was once used for people to check in, punch their time cards, and board the industrial cages that delivered them to the appropriate floor. Warehouses, by comparison, which were primarily used for storage and have little light or air as a consequence, seldom needed a separate entrance area, but did need loading bays for cargo.

Structural and service details help to define these spaces. Over-scaled, exposed industrial fixtures such as freight elevators, pipes and ducts, sprinkler valves, gilled radiators and fire escapes all reflect the former function of the building and are usually visible in the common areas. Whether to replace them, disguise them or make a feature of them is a question. In the ground-floor entrance to the late-nineteenth-century Melbourne factory, Peter Elliott deliberately

left the crumbling plaster-and-lathe ceiling, sandblasted brick walls, and industrial metal-framed doors. Well-worn soft pine stairs begin their ascent to emerge in the central first-floor vestibule, just below a double-hung Victorian window that overlooks an old brick lightwell. In this vestibule, ceiling

1 In a New York loft conversion the entrance is shielded from the open-plan kitchen by a large, pivoting industrial steel door on castors inset in a semicircular groove. Next to it a blond wood partition houses the library.

tie-rods that are a structural necessity have been retained – without them the building would fall down. Visitors are greeted with an immediate reference to the building's industrial heritage as well as a grand welcome. In another Australian conversion, Wayne Cross and Chris Malden's raw-brick 1940s warehouse conversion in Melbourne, designed by architect Ken Charles, the factory loading bay has been turned into a spacious entrance atrium beneath a glazed roof.

Fire regulations in Britain, which require the cooking area to be separated from the entrance area by a door, inspired an innovative entrance hall in a converted telephone exchange. Instead of simply boxing in the front entrance with a double layer of doors (a new front door, then a cell and another door), Jenny Armit and architect Mya Myanides surrounded the front door with

a semi-circular floor-to-ceiling partition wall that contains a door in the middle.

Unlike factories, farm buildings never featured formal entrances. The tractors – or the herd – were just driven straight in. The eighteenth-century New England pine barn that an American couple disassembled and shipped to the Santa Ynez vineyards in California, was designed with a central hall without divider walls, so the entrance hall naturally became part of the overall living space. Inside the front door they hung a Pennsylvania pediment.

In contrast, William Leddy's 1990s adaptation of the stainless-steel American grain silo attached to a wooden Pennsylvania barn, creates a separate defined entrance as well as a bathroom for the bedroom upstairs. Though the architect in this instance needed to create an entrance where none had existed, he adhered to the vernacular with wit and creativity – adding the cylindrical steel silo to a barn in which there were no longer any cattle. To make an agricultural building habitable and give the new inhabitants this more functional space, Leddy introduced metal posts and steel beams to carry the weight that the old stone walls could not support.

2 Plants and containers on the old fire escape of this conversion in east London make a decorative entrance, leading to the building's original fire-doors.

3 Fire regulations can often make planning the entrance difficult. Doors are required to block off the front door from open-plan living and cooking areas beyond. Metal panels grooved like quilting make a feature of this fire door in a New York apartment.

4 Relaxing

Furniture designer Gustav Stickley is America's answer to William Morris and the Arts and Crafts Movement. He defined his ideal house in 1900 as having plenty of free space, unencumbered by unnecessary partitions and with one big living room into which one steps directly from the front entrance. Unusually for a furniture-maker, he preferred the space without much furniture. A century later, he would have found his ideal in a loft. In converted residences as well as in purpose-built houses, the maximum amount of space is usually allotted to the living area, with other rooms – bedroom, bathroom, kitchen – limited by rational planning to the smallest reasonable size without sacrificing convenience. But even the best designers and architects sometimes have a problem with living spaces. Bathrooms and kitchens have clearly defined functions, while 'living' means different things to different people. Comfort, however, is a common denominator, and should always be a priority, with attention paid to seating, viewing, sound, warmth and light.

1 Relaxation in a converted power station in Texas is as easy as installing a grand piano and a sound system for the opera-loving owners. Architect Gary Cunningham has put fibreglass acoustic panels against the bare brick walls to help the sound system in the absence of any soft furniture. A single Charles Eames recliner and footstool are placed for the best listening.

1 Beneath the reinforced stainless-steel joists and floor-to-ceiling glass, colour creates a friendly space for cooking and relaxing. The partition wall has been cut into a ziggurat that is highlighted by the yellow panelling in the kitchen.

2 Modern speakers and a CD display unit are mounted against the brick wall to make a feature of the sound system.

3 Sometimes sight and sound systems need to be concealed. The owners of this apartment have had specially designed a modular unit with stainless-steel doors to hide speakers, television and stacked systems, while making the sophisticated CD player on its freestanding pedestal a sculptural object in the room.

Since most people spend the majority of their time at home in the living area, this is the space that needs to serve the largest variety of functions – from relaxing and enjoying music or television to entertaining. Whether you prefer several clustered seating areas in an open plan, or one large space to spread out in, a well-defined living space is a great asset.

Zoning the apartment is the first step. That old-fashioned focal point of most interior designs, a fireplace, will no longer govern the design of the living space if there is under-floor heating or under-window radiator cylinders. With no such limitations on seating plans, let daylight guide your placement of the living area. Even if you mainly inhabit the apartment at night, your weekends will be spent relaxing there and you might want to position sofas and chairs to take best advantage of natural light and the view, which at night in a city can be very exciting. Fashion entrepreneur Craig Port never screens the windows of his second-storey warehouse apartment in Cape Town because they frame Table Mountain, which is illuminated by night. If you watch television a lot you can still have a living area near the window, as long as you devise some way of shielding the screen or dimming the incoming light for good viewing.

You may want at least one external party wall in the living area as a support for shelves to hold books, CDs and videos, or you may want to site the living space in the core of the apartment and use free-standing towers instead. The television and video themselves can be kept on trolleys, so that they can be moved when and where needed.

Once the decision has been made as to where to position the main living area, separating it need not mean floor-to-ceiling walls which hamper movement and block light. Built-in or free-standing furniture can suggest boundaries; irregularly shaped, two-third-height partitions can close off an area. Folding screens of fabric, wood or paper on pivotal hinges will also act as partitions. If the living space is near a window-wall, you might want to block daylight at the windows with curtains or shutters.

Lighting designer André Tammes uses lighting to distinguish the different areas of his family home in a converted grain warehouse. Without subdivisions and barriers, the daylight streams in unbroken from windows on three sides of the living space, but Tammes has also devised a centrally controlled lighting system, creating pools of light to define separate areas.

Artificial light should be controlled by dimmer switches to suit your mood: bright and sparkly, or more intimate. General light, recessed in the ceiling or from spots overhead, will need backup from 'task' lighting at eye level. You may need a few tables for lamps in order to bring light down to a more human scale as well as to hold phones, papers, books and other items. Well-designed tabletops (what interior designer David Hicks has called 'tablescapes') become a decorative element when viewed from your platform bed on a mezzanine.

A change in surface finish or floor treatment can also denote a change in space. Acres of bare-brick party walls can be broken up by hanging a brilliant sari, like a banner, across the soaring background. A piece of fabric floating above sitting, dining and cooking areas can add definition and inspire a colour scheme. Underfoot, it works as well. Designer Willie Nickerson's use of rugs to make little oases, with clusters of sofas and tables dotted around a vast former classroom, defines

1 An old tractor shed in Kempsey, Australia, with tallow-wood walls and floors, has been converted by the architect Glenn Murcutt. The simplicity of the utilitarian background is retained in the custom-built kitchen units. Sophistication is introduced with modern leather furniture, an Alvar Aalto bent plywood 'Pamio' chair and the dining chairs by another Scandinavian, Arne Jacobsen.

2 The Liverpool-based, English architects Urban Splash, who worked on this old Smithfield warehouse in London, brought living space down to earth with a partition screen two-thirds of the way up to the ceiling. The lower level of the room is emphasized with squashy modern furniture.

3 Unusually, the owners of this New York apartment have used Arts and Crafts benches and chairs alongside a modern dining table and chairs. The grand piano that separates the living and dining areas crosses the divide between turn-of-the-century old and state-of-the-art new.

different seating areas without breaking up the sense of space. Dhurries and kilims in strong tones of nasturtium, purple, raspberry and Bristol blue neatly divide the ground-floor living room into four conversational groups.

Removing the limitations imposed by dividing walls can result in unconventional furniture arrangements. Centre-of-the-room furniture arrangements are the twenty-first-century equivalent of the old nineteenth-century salon – where chairs lined the walls and left the ballroom-sized centre free. Scale is important. Huge spaces are notoriously difficult to handle. Small pieces of furniture tend to get swallowed up, while larger ones look uneasily marooned, and a surfeit of furniture can produce a

room with all the less charming characteristics of an airport lounge. Yet the new purpose-built modular units originally launched as furniture for hotel foyers and airport lounges can be pushed together into many configurations. They introduce solid blocks of colour, and their dimensions suit big spaces.

Putting comfort high on the list of priorities need not negate a feeling of space and may improve the acoustics. Fibreglass panels,

1 This Pennsylvanian Dutch barn, built around 1820, has exposed steel joists on the ceiling and a stairwell that are echoed in the geometric design of the custom-made furniture.

2 The bulky columns of this building have inspired the choice of comfortable, capacious leather furniture and a central round coffee table on a column plinth.

3 Modular furniture with loose slipcovers and big cushions creates a friendly corner from which to look out of the rigorously delineated windows.

4 The living space below this mezzanine floor is illuminated by a folk-art-inspired chandelier by lighting designer André Tammes.

as smoothly shellacked as canoe shells and coloured to match soft furnishings, can help acoustics by reducing unfriendly echo. When converting a Victorian tea warehouse on the Thames in London, architect Tony Goddard found the white plaster walls and wooden floors too hard; so any new walls he created were covered in felt 'to make it cosy'. As well as the pattern and colour changes that soft furnishings introduce to a room, sofas, curtains and upholstered chairs all help to contain sound. You should therefore consider carefully the fixtures and furnishings in the area where you are likely to house the radio and the stack systems for CDs.

1 The hard surfaces of bare brick on one side and ceramic tiles on the other contain a comfortable living area with loose linen slipcovers on friendly, traditional furniture and a woven rug.

2 The artist Robert Indiana has an idiosyncratic style, cramming together furniture of many different periods and designs with graphic art (including his own) and rugs in many patterns and colours.

3 This conversion of an eighteenth-century Dutch barn in the Hamptons was furnished by Gwathmey Siegel of New York. He used a combination of turn-of-the-twentieth-century folk-art chairs, modern three-seater soft-upholstered sofas, and a pair of ceramic-tiled tables to build upon the geometry of the existing structure. A tall, rustic cupboard takes the eye upwards towards a pair of carved wooden decoy ducks displayed on the top.

Tea Warehouse, London

Reflections on the Thames

Oliver's Wharf is a protected London landmark on the River Thames, pointed out in the commentaries of the tour guides whose ferries ply the river. The handsome waterfront tea warehouse was built in 1870 by the Oliver family. A hundred years later it was one of the first loft-block conversions to take place in London. The bohemian spirit of the pioneers and their adventurous attitude can still be glimpsed in the hammocks, herb boxes and windchimes framed in the windows. However, by the 1990s some of the conversions had started to look dated. Two young British-based architects, Jonathan McDowell and Renato Benedetti, have achieved a handsome conversion in one of them – a rooftop apartment, owned by an architectural enamellist who lives and works there.

When Renato Benedetti first saw the apartment, it was unoccupied and had been gutted by the previous owner, Lord Palumbo, a champion of the modern movement. What was left – woodwork and bare brick – was rustic rather than metropolitan in feel: 'Like a big dilapidated country barn,' Renato Benedetti recalls. The new owner wanted an open-plan living space (3) that emphasized the river

views, as well as the natural light and its reflections. The architects shared his enthusiasms.

McDowell and Benedetti drew up a plan for renovating the 232sq.m (2,500sq.ft), double-height space, introducing cast-iron columns supporting oak trusses under a pitched roof (3, 4). They determined to increase the space, now 372sq.m (4,000sq.ft), by adding a new top level and roof terraces, and took advantage of the high ceiling to build a mezzanine floor. The first step was to carry out extensive repairs. They were astonished to find no fire protection between apartments. Planning permission had been granted for a rooftop conservatory, but the more modest design they proposed in its place was gratefully endorsed by English Heritage and the London Docklands Development Corporation.

On the riverfront there is no problem with being overlooked by neighbouring buildings. With an unobstructed view of the river and Tower Bridge, sunsets on the western aspect are spectacular. A new bedroom was created on the mezzanine level, with a fully glazed shower-room extending out onto the roof, which has panoramic views of London. Now that the project is complete, they all agree that one of the most satisfying bonuses has proved to be the reflections from the river, which, even on the fifth floor, play upon the ceilings, due to the skilful manipulation of light through the three open levels of the interior.

Stripped back to the bare brick shell and wooden beams, without ceilings or partitions, the apartment is well-proportioned. Creating the main division within the open volume is a three-storey-high Spanish limestone wall, 20cm (8in) thick, running down the centre of the interior. The fine-grained, light-coloured stone anchors the luminous space and reflects light down from the cast-glass seats above. The wall is backed with cupboards upstairs and storage and service cupboards at kitchen-level downstairs. A guest bedroom – which doubles as a studio – and two bathrooms are contained behind a white plastered wall with a door that is usually kept open to encourage freedom of movement throughout the space.

'Crisply detailed modern elements transform the old shell'
RENATO BENEDETTI

3

The new mezzanine bedroom/bathroom, terrace and rooftop additions were carefully integrated with the original building. The walls were sandblasted to give the bare brick a mellow glow. New surfaces were chosen to contrast with the existing fabric: limestone for the three-storey-high dividing wall and sandblasted steel for the new two-storey-high fireplace screen, which has been surface welded and contains not only the gas fire but also bookshelves, a seat and, above, a sink for the studio. This screen also conceals a secret steel stairway to the studio, and supports the solid oak studio floor. Throughout the apartment, intensely coloured enamelled steel screens and cupboard doors by Vera Ronnen and the owner are judiciously placed to reflect the natural light.

Complementing these materials are floorboards of English oak in broad planks, below which run underfloor heating and an acoustic insulation mat.

The original steel windows were replaced with double-glazed oak-framed units retaining the old design (6). New openings for the bedroom terrace and the glazed rooftop addition were framed in steel to differentiate them from the original building. The windows and skylights, glazed sections and internal glass walls are designed to keep light beaming into the core of the apartment across three floors. By day the whole space is bathed in a luminous, watery light. Hidden artificial lights, placed along the skylights, ensure that by night, light comes down from the same direction. Dimmer controls can be preset or overridden manually. Even the staircase is designed to pass light down through the space.

Constructed from folded plates of shot-blasted steel, it climbs around a central screen of translucent cast-glass slabs (1), lit during the day via the rooflight above and at night by concealed uplighters in the floor below.

Glass is the medium best suited to this illuminated space. A special cast-glass mix, made up by Jeff Bell to the architectural duo's designs, was used for continuous parallel linear skylights (2, 4) which allow light to bathe the apartment. 'The textured green glass with entrapped bubbles looks like melting ice,' Renato Benedetti says. Even the basin in the middle of the main bedroom is a cast-glass bowl on a polished aluminium base. Taps and lighting are concealed in a mirrored cabinet above it. Cast-glass slabs are everywhere: even in the shower screen and the seats suspended above the floor voids around the roof extensions.

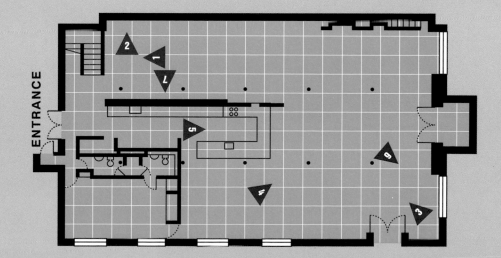

The architects specifically tailored design has created a highly individual apartment within a complex existing context. They have used innovative structural solutions to introduce new architectural elements and open up panoramic views over London. Specially designed glass seating lines the rooftop terrace and allows maximum natural light into the interior. Unusual materials such as solid limestone blocks, sandblasted raw steel, Japanese lacquer, solid oak, stainless steel and hand-made cast glass have been carefully selected to contrast with the existing textures of the rough brick warehouse.

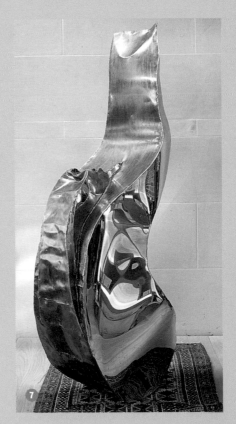

4 Cooking & Eating

Site the kitchen before you choose the kind of kitchen fixtures and appliances, as mistakes even at this early stage are expensive to rectify. The easiest and most cost-effective installations are near the existing gas and electricity supplies, or near the oil tank in a country location. Hot- and cold-water supply taps and an outside soil-stack outlet where the sink water will drain, along with water from the bath, shower, toilet, handbasin, dishwasher and washing machine, will determine the position of sinks and washing appliances. The sink should not be more than 2.3m (7$\frac{1}{2}$ft) from the waste outlet. Some lofts are well served with these plumbing essentials, but others need to have them added or refurbished.

If access to gas, water and electricity is not where you want to site the kitchen, you can consider alternative ways to install new pipes and wiring, which are usually run under the floorboards. Cabling for overhead lighting in the kitchen and dining area, which allows the chef to work comfortably and diners to enjoy meals, also needs to be built in early.

In a former insurance office building, architect Barrie Legg found that the heavy concrete floors, walls and ceilings of his 121sq.m (1,304sq.ft) apartment were difficult to work with. He

1 This industrial makeover in Princeton, New Jersey, betrays no sign of its origins as a brick factory. Shop fixtures in wire and steel, slate slabs and stainless-steel industrial chef's appliances are used to create a kitchen work-station that is more laboratory than conventional kitchen

2 Industrial designer Ross Lovegrove designed and moulded his kitchen sinks from carbon fibre. They have shallow ribs allowing water to drain into the two sinks, which are at different levels.

3 A feature is made of a former industrial duct, focusing interest above a central-island cooking unit in this New York loft.

4 In this otherwise open-plan conversion of a former power station in Texas, Gary Cunningham used a translucent screen to separate off the kitchen area.

could not place the utilities where he wanted them. So he ran the wiring and pipes for gas, electricity and television through a fake ceiling beam, made to look identical to those that were already there. In effect, he turned the project upside down, working around the beams from the ceiling, rather than trying to incorporate the utilities into a floor plan.

Architect Michael Rubins glamorized an industrial space of 232sq.m (2,500sq.ft) in a Manhattan printing plant for his family of four by siting the kitchen in the centre. 'To the children on their bikes and skates, the home is just one big piazza,' he says. With windows wrapping around the shell on three sides, natural light was not a problem and Rubins maintains that once they decided to make the kitchen the core, everything else just fell into place. To reinforce that piazza image, he laid pink marble flooring in the kitchen and dining area.

Ventilation is the other important consideration when siting the kitchen. In most loft conversions the ventilation hood takes the place of the traditional hearth. Fortunately, most former industrial buildings have extensive ducting in their high ceilings so that cooking hoods can draw condensation and cooking smells to the outside.

Whether you choose to build your kitchen yourself or have unit systems installed, make a simple sketch showing the shape, length, width and height of the proposed site. Draw the windows and doors to scale and in their correct positions. To determine the possible configurations, gas and water pipes, electrical sockets and ventilation should also be shown. Standard units for kitchen cupboards, sinks, wall display and food storage are not sized for industrial pipes and ducts, and trying to fit a standard-sized modular unit – which will have pre-cut notches at the back to accommodate the plumbing – in an overscaled industrial refit will not work. So a sketch with measurements is vital.

❶ Architects Peter Forbes & Associates used rectangular and semi-circular surfaces to partition the cooking and dining space within this open-plan loft conversion in Rhode Island.

❷ A high-sided breakfast bar covered in big grey ceramic tiles screens the cooking area, hides clutter and creates an interesting backdrop for a round glass table and 1950s vinyl chairs.

❸ A long, stainless-steel custom-built worktop with inset cooking area creates a horizontal kitchen opening out to a T-line dining area, a configuration that is enhanced by the table on castors and Arne Jacobsen chairs.

❹ A bank of stainless-steel wire shopfitting storage is stacked floor to ceiling to create a transparent partition that doubles as plate rack and, with butcher's hooks, utensil storage for a kitchen.

There are two basic kitchen styles. First is the freestanding kitchen, in which you freely combine different new or reclaimed pieces: a butcher's block, a wire-mesh-fronted larder for dried goods on either side of an oven and refrigerator, and a double butler sink with groovy taps and exposed plumbing flanked by worktops on wheels. Or, where suitable in size, the built-in, fitted kitchen can be installed. This has a run of brand-name units, in which the

In addition to a sketch, also consider and list extra kitchen-storage items that may require alteration to the units – for example, horizontal steel rails with butcher's hooks, tiered mesh vegetable baskets, a rubbish bin, pot-lid racks, utensil trays, mixer taps at a round or square sink, wine shelf and storage jars. Only then should you shop for the cabinet frames, door panels, plinths or legs and work-tops that will hold them.

Small or large, central free-standing or tucked into a corner, the kitchen in an open-plan conversion is always on display. Conventional appliances can look underscaled in a loft space, which is why industrial equipment is often used. Appliances are often bigger and more assertive, enamelled bright yellow or blue,

or bow-fronted in stainless steel. Since the refrigerator today has had to replace both the pantry and the larder, it is deservedly the biggest container in the kitchen area. The micro-wave, the chef's industrial oven, or the Aga or Viking stove, which still reigns in rural areas, all have a presence. So does the American stainless-steel cooker, which is the perfect complement to the chrome Dualit toaster and an Italian espresso machine. When *Vogue* magazine photo-graphed American fashion designer Isaac Mizrahi at home in 1996, he didn't get nearly as much attention as his cooker, a home-on-the-range stainless-steel Viking. These ovens can chargrill a tuna steak in one minute, but they need powerful ventilators and a well-maintained flue to prevent meltdown.

1 The contrast of textures, from pebble-dash stones set into cement as a plinth support, to stainless-steel-fronted worktops, stone worksurfaces and splashbacks, and a steel hearth set against white plastered walls, forms interesting juxtapositions in this kitchen.

2 The sliding horizontal partitions create a geometric, L-shaped kitchen in the middle of this New York loft and were the inspiration for the backlit panels on the edges of the unit, which reinforce the Japanese look.

3 The kitchen area here is enclosed by a simple, freestanding front with cupboards and a serving hatch so that the cook's clutter can be cleared away when necessary.

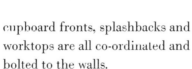

cupboard fronts, splashbacks and worktops are all co-ordinated and bolted to the walls.

Taut steel designer tables can be combined with chefs' stainless-steel ovens, and bow-fronted double-doored fridges big enough to feed a banquet. Or you can opt for a stripped pine flat-pack kitchen with standardized units and appliances, spice and wine racks and a refectory table. There are designer kitchens that feature wire-mesh-and-glass-fronted cupboards, patinated metal, polished stone and backlit glass units, perhaps complementing a breakfast bar and leggy Barcelona bar stools. Mix-and-match materials from wood to steel can be combined with granite, marble or teak splashbacks and worktops. Whatever the look, these New Age kitchens combine personal creativity with function.

On the freestanding front, Eurocucine, the annual Milan kitchen show, constructed a kitchen from as few as three separate pieces: a big rectangular table that houses an oven below the work surface and a hob (burners) on the table-top, accessorized by a huge silver-nozzled ventilation hood; a double sink set in a second matching tabletop that contains filing cabinet drawers for utensils; and a huge pantry on industrial castors with concertina fold-in doors. Freestanding kitchen pieces with legs on industrial rollers allow for maximum mobility and can easily be moved to reconfigure the space.

If you are able to buy ready-made units you can always customize them. Architect Alf Munkenbeck takes standard pine units and fits them with stainless-steel

worktops and splashbacks. Interior designer Jenny Armit spray-paints them with a metallic finish and then designs overscaled handles in interesting cut-outs for the door fronts. Ralph Ardill of the Imagination Gallery in London, who lives in a converted watch-maker's factory, keeps his open-plan kitchen neat behind coloured MDF panels. Julian Metcalfe cut his furnishing budget to spend more on custom-building his kitchen at one end of a former classroom, covering MDF panels with burnished steel. This is also the signature of Prêt à Manger, his chain of sandwich bar/coffee shops, which extend throughout Britain.

Your own kitchen can be as small or large, as professional or as simple as your personality dictates. Architect Brian Ma Siy and his wife Anke love cooking and do a lot of it, so they planned their kitchen around the appliances they needed. First they sited the kitchen in the middle of their schoolhouse conversion in south London. They chose a six-ring gas hob (burner) because they prefer wok and griddle cooking, and the simple single oven because they do not use it often. They measured the largest plate they owned and bought shelves to fit those dimensions. There is no dining table in the room, just two sitting areas and a stainless-steel worktop where they prepare the food, eat and entertain.

Not everyone wants to turn professional cook. Tyne O'Connell, the Australian author of the novel *Latest Accessories*, which is about a band of It Girls living in a loft with a collection of erotica, admits that her own kitchen in a converted pipe factory in London is not one that she can actually cook in. There is a sink, a cappuccino machine, and a larder improvised from a grey metal filing cabinet. Some second-hand dining chairs and a wrought-iron candelabra are sprayed with silver car paint to tie in with the industrial look. 'We eat a lot of sushi,' O'Connell admits. 'It's like an eternal picnic. It is what living in the city is all about.' Also for a more specialized palate, architect

1 In a show flat for a London loft near Kings Cross station, interior designer Jenny Armit did not have the option of moving the kitchen, because the service areas for water and electricity backed onto the bathroom. To maximize light in the inner core she installed three opaque windows and painted the partition walls on either side deep blue to identify the cooking area. In the open-plan living and dining space, shop fixtures and IKEA units stack under a simple wooden worktop, which leaves the plumbing for the double sinks exposed. Two workstations, one with a steel top and the other with a wooden surface, are on castors and can be moved around.

2 Graphic designer Luigi Ferrario has created a kitchen for a bachelor under the stairs of his Lombardy home. A single hob (burner) is flanked on either side by two worktops, one in slate and one in wood, which double as a dining area.

3 The kitchen as laboratory is seen in a converted cinema in Scotland, the home of Bob Callender and Liz Ogilvie. Everything a cook needs is at hand in a wire trolley, and an industrial ventilator is situated above the cooking area.

Mark Guard fitted a teriyaki bar for sizzle cuisine in a loft conversion above the famously busy Mezzo restaurant in London's Soho.

If the kitchen is a place for creativity and self-expression, the dining area is a place for interaction. Loft or barn conversions seldom separate and close off the dining area, but dining areas that are open to the rest of the space may need to be given boundaries. Breakfast bars break up a grid of columns and joists to define a space for cooking and eating and allow for more circulation in open-plan living. Tracks that run through the middle of a 279sq.m (3,000sq.ft) packing plant at New Concordia Wharf, London, were gouged out by the

architect Mark Guard because his client did not want his dining area to be restricted to one location. In fact there are two tables set into the stainless-steel tracks on spring-loaded roller bearings. One table, a slab of green glass on slim, steel legs, is for eating at, the other, with a more practical stainless-steel surface, rolls towards the dining table loaded like a supply wagon.

Dining tables and chairs naturally end up near the food-preparation area. But not in the home of career woman Laurence Kriegel, a mother of five who lives in an old chocolate factory in New York. Though the kitchen-diner at the central core of this busy household is used for family meals, she chose to site a

separate smaller dining area in the defunct water tank on the rooftop of her adjoining SoHo design shop, for friends and business associates who lunch with her. Within the industrial space, she has divided her life between her work and her family.

The table can become a design statement, as evidenced in graphic designer Tessa Priestman's bare-brick-and-boards former garage. She covered hers with builders' dustsheets. Fibrous, chalky white, disposable and tough, these table-cloths are outlined with place settings when Tessa swiftly sketches a knife, fork and spoon in black ink before laying the table. Such a spontaneous gesture helps to create a sense of welcome.

4 Sleeping

In the opening shots of the film *Ghost* a young couple consider rearranging their fashionable but gritty loft conversion. Demi Moore peers up into the eaves to gulp, 'It's got to be seven or eight feet up there.'

'And 80 years of dust,' Patrick Swayze replies.

'We can put the bed upstairs and that leaves us with all that space,' Demi says.

'Space for what?'

'Just space.'

'Just space' is probably the most luxurious concept for a bedroom that any of us can imagine. In today's homes, the living room given the largest space, while the bedroom is shoe-horned into the smallest. Bedrooms in modern houses are seldom larger than 3.7 x 3m (12 x 10ft). Put a double bed into that space, add a chest of drawers and a wardrobe (closet), and you have to get dressed somewhere else. So, in an industrial or agricultural conversion where you have open space, hijacking the mezzanine floor above all the action in the living quarters is a smart move. Now you will have a vantage point from which to survey everything while keeping your privacy.

Privacy and light are two important elements to explore when planning where to put down your mattress — more important than putting up walls and plugging in lamps. Privacy without rooms can be

achieved by elevating the bed beyond the sight line on the mezzanine level. For a sleeping area on the same level as the living space, use screens. These might be as monumental as a wall or as flimsy as a drape.

Too much light where you intend to sleep is as much of a problem as too little where you don't. Not wanting to reduce the amount of light or the view in his open-plan conversion of a Cape Town warehouse, fashion entrepreneur Craig Port gives airline eye masks to guests who spend the night, while interior designer Willie Nickerson found a more dramatic solution to the same problem in a converted Victorian school. When Nickerson removed the false ceiling in the London schoolhouse to expose the glazed mansard

1 Fashion entrepreneur Craig Port found a creative solution to the problem of providing comfortable guest accommodation. His dislike of blinds and curtains means that much of his warehouse conversion in Cape Town is flooded with light. A hospital bed on wheels allows guests to move the bed away from the windows, while airline eye masks prevent the dawn from intruding.

2 The high windows in this conversion in Toronto are a clue to the building's former incarnation as a dairy. Sited along the top of the wall, small windows were necessary to keep the interior cool and dark. Retaining the original features, architects Third Uncle Design have made the most of available light with a monochrome scheme. The mirror propped on the floor cleverly replicates the style of the windows.

roof, he had to devise a means of blocking the light coming into the top-floor bedroom without rigging electronic blinds. So he designed a four-poster bed on a 60cm (2ft) platform and canopied it with scaffolding hung with 70m (229ft) of inky blue and gold fabric. Scaled like a room within the open space, the scaffolding leaves a 91cm (3ft) walkway around the bed, and there is not a glimmer of light within.

Photographer Crena Watson framed her bedhead in a former schoolhouse by building a wall that stops just short of the beam high overhead. Flanked by the wall of the adjoining bathroom, with its

grid of backlit glazed panels like lightboxes beamed onto her bed, it is both sheltered and illuminated.

A more transient solution is the Union Jack flag that stylist Katie England, of the magazine *Dazed and Confused*, hung to screen her bed in the 139sq.m (1,500sq.ft) open space that she inhabits in an old post office. In the old dairy that John Stefanidis converted into a country retreat, his bedroom has a backdrop of striped curtains to hide pitted masonry, and natural linen blinds loosely looped at the small windows to stay in keeping with the rustic charm. London-based furniture designer Daniel

Reynolds, who lives in a converted warehouse on the Thames, created a two-tiered sleeping area next to the windows by stringing up a hammock from the rafters and laying his mattress on the wooden floor. Now his choice of bed depends on his mood.

Sleeping soundly in a converted industrial building doesn't mean futons on the floor. Load-bearing floors can take a huge and heavy bed, and substantial pieces can take the place of sheltering walls or enclosures. Even if the rest of the apartment is furnished in a contemporary style, the self-important beds of another century are sometimes chosen over their more streamlined contemporary counterparts: baroque beds, *bateaux lits*, sleigh beds, Biedermeier beds, four-posters, iron truckle (trundle) beds, or beds with headboards and footboards. Knitwear designers Patrick and Jane Gottelier, who live in a converted sugar warehouse on the Thames in London, have a headboard constructed from a carved

mahogany overmantel like the crest of a wave, which they think came from a church. To dress it, they cable-knitted a cashmere cover and throws, pillow slips and cushion covers.

Dressing the bed can be an exercise in theatrical excess or white-linen restraint, for two very distinctive looks. A former office with a builder's yard, converted by ceramicist Kate Malone and Graham Inglefield into their three-storeyed home, has a carved wooden four-poster from Lombok in Indonesia canopied with an Indian tent. Inside, hang small brass birds, the sun, moon and stars. The tented room gives privacy without partitions.

For a more minimalist look, in a converted North Yorkshire school-room, Greville Worthington opted for a high-sided bed made from elm. The effect is a bit like sleeping in a three-sided, draught-free carton. He admits that the design was inspired by the minimalist sculptor Donald Judd. Sparsely but finely furnished with gauzy drapes on curling wrought-iron rails, made by the blacksmith Joe Cassell, it is an architectonic piece. And so is James Hong's bed in a Lower East Side loft in New York, which is screened by parachute nylon tinted in pastel hues and suspended from custom-built curved steel tubes positioned about 46cm (18in) from the windows.

1 Under the eaves in a barn conversion, a single partition two-thirds of the way across the pitched roof shields the bed from the stairs.

2 In this barn an army-surplus mosquito net screens the bed.

3 Although this bedroom has been partitioned from the dressing-room area, the owners decided not to cut the light, and installed a corrugated acrylic panel that diffuses both natural and artificial light.

4 The bedroom at the end of a long, open-plan living space is shielded simply by hanging muslin curtains from the rafters to the floor. On the opposite wall, ropes from the rafters support a hanging rail for clothes.

1 **2** To maximize light at the core of this New York loft apartment, a window-wall separates the sleeping and bathing areas from the cooking and living areas. Architects Hanrahan Meyers built the horizontal stacking glass wall with narrow glazing bars and introduced plain white cotton curtains on their own inset track to pull back like a concertina screen. A different view of the sleeping area with the curtains drawn back shows how the geometric design makes the most use of space and light.

3 A special headboard, built for the William Leddy barn in Pennsylvania, has task lights for reading under the dimly lit eaves.

Although loft-dwellers like old beds for their awesome size and presence, there is not much call for period-piece storage – clumsy wardrobes and bow-fronted chests of drawers. Old office furniture or recycled industrial equipment efficiently matches the needs of inhabitants who move their clothes into compartments in metal filing cabinets or pigeonholes, and use steel clothes rails and iron coat-stands. In her conversion of a wine warehouse on the Thames, magazine editor and top photographic stylist Sue Skeen used a combination of tin stacking trunks labelled for jerseys, socks and shirts with a freestanding

armoire featuring white tongue-and-groove doorfronts, which look like pallets with simple clasps.

Bedside lighting can be as simple as wall sconces if the bed is positioned against a party wall, or table lamps, in which case you might want two matched pieces (perhaps wine casks or packing crates) to hold them.

What kind of bedroom storage is needed will depend on where you make your sleeping area. You could use a platform bed to create a split-level effect, or an architectonic piece like Richard and Ruth Rogers'

canary-yellow multi-functional bed-cum-storage-and-library unit that makes the most of soaring spaces. This custom-made bed is fitted with shelves and drawers at the back of the head-board, and plinths on either side, which hold books and double as bedside tables with built-in lighting so that the bed functions as an entire bedroom.

Whatever its history, a converted barn or factory building was probably never plumbed to have a bathroom, so you start with no heritage. Siting it depends on what services are available, so bathrooms often end up in the most extraordinary places. Bathers in Tyne O'Connell's converted pipe factory soak in the rolltop bath beside a spiral staircase that leads to the rooftop garden. Architect John Young, of Richard Rogers Partnership, has a penthouse bath and shower. A girdle of tubular stainless steel carries both plumbing and heating pipes, and frames the glass bricks that encircle the bathing space. The bath is a sunken cedarwood Japanese tub and is sealed by a slab of wood when not in use.

If there is only one door in your newly converted industrial space, other than the front door, it will inevitably lead to the bathroom, and this means having a wall of some kind. One of the most audacious solutions is Mark Guard's electrochromic glass panel that can turn opaque. Guard uses it to screen the bathroom that is situated just off the living area. When the bathroom is occupied, the molecule-coated glass can be changed from clear to cloudy.

In their steel-frame and glass two-floor extension above a flower workshop, florist Paula Pryke and her husband, architect Peter

1. **2** The sensitive use of lighting and fixtures in interesting materials can make the bathroom an oasis in the mêlée of a larger space. A roof light and slot windows on either side of a deep-soak tub create an austerely monastic bathroom. The skylight, in another, causes a flattering overhead light to fall on a glass basin.

3 In a large open loft, a partition wall encloses a modern bathroom, where the flooring intrudes into the living area like a bath mat, leading the eye between the rooms. The mirror and basin-top create horizontal lines in pleasing contrast to the tall verticals of the space outside.

Romaniuk, screened their cast-iron rolltop bath, basin and shower area from the glass façade with three semicircles of blue-and-white canvas rigged like sails. Three circular glass skylights bathe the tub, the shower and the basin area in natural light. Peter Romaniuk made what he calls 'the shower tree' fitting this into a single upright pipe that stands like a column next to the bath. It has stainless-steel cooking utensils, taps and stopcocks, a round shaving mirror and a shower nozzle.

Another solution that frees bathing from behind closed doors was developed in a converted electrical warehouse by Future Systems, a husband-and-wife team of architects, who installed an architectonic piece of brightly coloured MDF that hides the bath behind a spiralling partition that stops far short of the ceiling height. In his designs for the Royalton Hotel in New York, Philippe Starck used a wall of opaque glass bricks that curves partway around the tub and encloses it in a semicircle. To complete the cylinder, a shower curtain hangs from a semicircular chrome rail. The bathroom is also a wall-free zone in architects Jane Tankard and Steve Bowkett's 1930s clothing factory in Nile Street, London, where they have shielded the bath behind an opaque glass panel set into a brick partition.

1 If plumbing essentials permit a freestanding, centrally placed shower, a curved glass cubicle such as this could be installed. The water pipes have been clad in metal to look like pillars and also support ceramic basins.

▶ *Clockwise from top left*: in a basement conversion the shower has been placed below street level, and is shielded by a glass door; opaque griddled glass lets in natural light. This marbled stone sink has its original taps, and makes a novel feature in a converted barn. Luigi Ferrario's stone-walled Lombardy house has a hand-held shower and a shallow-inset, reinforced-glass basin with a modern sliding screen door. In this dairy conversion, white skim-plastered walls surround a sunken bath which is fed by a very modern angular tube tap.

If the bathroom is enclosed behind walls, there are ways to make it more interesting. Stuart Parr's enormous New York loft bathroom has white-painted tongue-and-groove boards that extend two-thirds of the way up the wall to wrap around the room. High above, the original air ducts and ancient pipes are visible, but the plumbing servicing the new fixtures is hidden in the panelling. The enclosed room is furnished with a pristine white corner sink on an Edwardian pedestal with ceramic splashback, a porcelain toilet, chrome hardware and a stainless-steel mirror. Hovering above this white installation, the cavernous old roof, traversed with piping and ventilation equipment, is a reminder of the building's industrial origins. Architect Kees van der Sande had much the same film-set approach to a London loft

in a 1930s building that had been a warehouse for the rag trade. He removed the polystyrene (styrofoam) ceiling and installed a glass roof above the shower. Opaque glass sliding panels screen the toilet.

An extension is an ideal way to add a bathroom. Adding on to a converted structure is a luxury afforded to those owning the land surrounding a conversion. In Melbourne, Australia, architects Julie Meacham and Don McQuatter were able to make a small addition to their warehouse conversion to house a sunken bath that can accommodate four bathers. The new structure is long and narrow like a railway carriage with floor-to-ceiling cupboards to separate it from the bedroom next door. The bathtub is tiled in blue mosaic, and the other three surrounding walls are rubbed with coloured pigment.

Big bathrooms in conversions can take an oversized and unconventional bath. No longer limited to a standard-sized built-in utilitarian unit, residents can literally splash out on bathtubs that are freestanding, rectangular or round, or corner baths enclosed in panelling. As bathtubs have to be fitted with pipework inlets and drainage, they are traditionally panelled, but the panelling material need not be wood; it could just as well be corrugated metal. Colourful bathroom suites, reminiscent of the 1970s, with corner bathtubs, clumsy showerheads and little vanity basins in matching shapes and colours not only look wrong in a voluminous industrial space, but they fail to take any advantage of the free-form possibilities. Architect Jan Kaplicky so liked the skeletal struts supporting a moulded fibreglass and enamelled white bathtub that,

1 In the dimly lit inner core of a packaging factory in Chicago, curved glass bricks and white tiles create a shower cubicle that diffuses the light while maintaining privacy.

2 The water pipes that feed this old cast-iron bathtub have been concealed in a tiled wall that creates a shower cubicle on the other side. The shower has been sloped for drainage.

3 A tiled installation under the eaves of an old barn creates a thoroughly modern bathroom for two, with the comfort at foot level of a large industrial radiator.

instead of adding panelling to hide the structural frame, he just put legs on it. Many loft-dwellers choose a classic rolltop tub, even if they do paint it scarlet, stand it on seagrass and draw up a shocking pink upholstered chair, as fabric designer Carol Thomas did behind the imposing façade of a converted bank in the City of London.

1 The vaulted walls and windows of this bathroom suggested the period fixtures.

2 A crimson bathtub and baroque furnishings in a London pop video producer's schoolhouse conversion take on a surreal look when set against the bare brick and sandblasted patina of the original wall surfaces.

3 The high floor-to-ceiling space in this former factory in London prompted owners Tim and Carol Wood to build a deep platform in the bedroom. They then inset a bathtub at the foot of the cast-iron spiral staircase and gave it a marble surround on the wooden deck.

Although Philippe Starck's triangular glass basin, which uses infra-red sensors to switch on the water flow so that it fills as the bather approaches, has yet to be put into domestic production, his deep tubs and pail basins on a pedestal are designed and manufactured to be freestanding. His Shaker-like shapes, produced in matt white, and used in large white-walled bathrooms with plain wood floors, have a pleasing austerity.

Bathtubs are positioned according to drainage access. But accessories like salvaged hospital washstands and lockers that were designed to be pulled along corridors offer flexibility. That's the idea behind architect Ron Arad's design for Italian glass manufacturers Fiam, which incorporates glass trolleys set on industrial aluminium castors like airport steps. The sides are of corrugated glass, into which fit reinforced wood and glass shelving strong enough to hold the television and video for bath-time viewing.

When fitting out a bathroom in a converted space, there are some general rules to consider. Surface finishes in bathrooms should be enduring and imper-meable. The best are glass and ceramic, concrete and marble, wood and stone. In a large area, avoid the small tiles that will take an expert tiler ages to grout. Keep to the big picture.

Underfloor heating is the best system for the bathroom, as it is efficient and takes up no space.

A more basic, but expensive, solution was used by architect Pip Horne, who lined bathroom floors in a converted fruit-market warehouse in biscuit-coloured Roman sandstone because it is naturally warm underfoot.

If you start from scratch in a factory, warehouse or barn, there is nothing to deter you from using contemporary designs like the tiles created by the Dutch design team Droog for Rosenthal ceramics. Steel soap drawers panelled with a single-coloured

ceramic tile pull out of a recess in a tiled shower wall. Floor tiles have water-drop finishes frozen in clear glass like droplets. Duncan Chapman of Circus Architects used coloured, smoothly varnished fibreglass panels to line the walls of the shower room he built in a con-version in an old brick printworks.

For those accustomed to the cramped shower stalls of purpose-built homes, the opportunity to create a sybaritic experience in a converted space is a major appeal.

4 Working

Loft living, defined as the conversion of industrial space into living and working space, began when artists moved into warehouses in New York and Paris. Sculptors cast bronzes in their backyards, ceramicists set up kilns, and glass blowers kept design workshops on the ground floor of their homes in these voluminous buildings which were cheap to rent and restore because they were derelict. Artists still inhabit these spaces. Yet the gentrification of former industrial buildings that occurred throughout the 1980s, referred to scornfully by modernists as 'lofties for softies', meant that once again these buildings fell silent by day as the homeowners went out to work.

Not any more. The changing technology that emptied these buildings in the first place is now turning

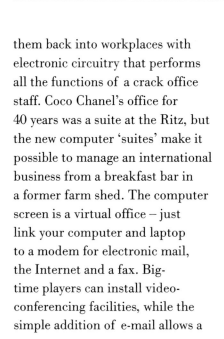

them back into workplaces with electronic circuitry that performs all the functions of a crack office staff. Coco Chanel's office for 40 years was a suite at the Ritz, but the new computer 'suites' make it possible to manage an international business from a breakfast bar in a former farm shed. The computer screen is a virtual office – just link your computer and laptop to a modem for electronic mail, the Internet and a fax. Big-time players can install video-conferencing facilities, while the simple addition of e-mail allows a

1 Architect Nico Rensch purpose-built this small folding worktop with swivelling side panels in a London loft.

2 A more permanent structure using drums as support for steel box-filing cabinets creates a worktop with an adjoining computer desk in this open-plan factory conversion in Belgium, owned by photographer Frank Destrooper.

3 On the mezzanine floor of this purpose-built freestanding cubicle is a study that takes advantage of natural light from the top of the kitchen window. Below is a kitchen storage cupboard specially designed by Circus Architects for a London couple who left their conventional suburban house when their children had grown up and moved away from home.

1 Barbara De Vries, fashion stylist, has sliding doors to her workplace. On one side are personal photographs, books, magazines and china, on the other is her equipment for pattern-cutting.

2 Fashion designer Jean Colonna, who lives in a former shoe factory in Paris, has made a flexible workplace simply by propping up a wooden pallet as a screen, stacking some wooden storage boxes and moving in mobile shopfitting units to house his books, magazines and drawing materials.

3 George Whiteside is a fashion photographer working from his home in a converted Toronto factory. He develops his negatives next to the kitchen sink.

4 Paula Iacucci has created a library and workplace in a New York loft. On one side is a wooden partition, and on the other a sliding screen, which can be moved to let in natural light.

staff writer for a communications company to live in Cyprus, yet put in daily working hours with his London office. 'It hasn't affected our working relationship,' comments his marketing manager, 'though I am sure it has affected the quality of his life.' All over the world, by accident or choice, workers once again work from home.

When home is a huge former industrial building without walled rooms, the first decision is whether to screen off a separate space in which to work, or to share the open-plan living with your office.

It is an important decision because it will affect how much your work becomes integrated with your domestic life. Working from home should not entail a kitchen or living space being taken over by computers and paperwork.

Creating a separate work area involves either building a study or sealing off part of the space. Sue and Paul Vaight, who exchanged life in a semi-detached (duplex) house for a rigorously modern warehouse conversion, bought two apartments in an old printing plant, and, with the help of Duncan Chapman of Circus Architects, knocked them together to form one vast open-living floor where they installed a cylindrical steel tower. This freestanding structure in the middle of the living area houses walk-in storage for the kitchen on the lower level and a study on top.

Even if it is a corner of the open-plan living room, the workplace needs special furnishing to equip the occupant to 'go to work' psychologically. Geoff Hollington, the furniture designer of contract installations for the American office company Herman Miller, believes that people working from home need to work in a special place, with a proper comfortable chair, a computer with its own desk, and with adequate storage for files. He has therefore designed a selection of office furniture that fits into the domestic environment and is especially suited to the flexible spaces in a conversion. Hollington's range of furniture has cabinets that look like sideboards but hold files inside, and tables with legs that are designed to contain cables.

Alternatively, using equipment that doubles as furniture can make the transition from work to relaxing easier. When Sue Skeen lived in a former wine warehouse, she shared her open-plan living with her work. Liking flexibility, she kept the magazines that inspired and informed her in

big wooden square trolleys with sliding tray shelves. The wooden work table was on castors and a bunch of old white stackable slatted metal chairs made it easy to host an impromptu meeting – or dinner party – for twelve. She used an angled standard lamp with an aluminium shade to cast direct light where needed.

As more people work from home, new designs in furnishings help to make a comfortable living environment and functional office in the same space.

Since technology frees us from the office, there is no reason to remain tied to the city centre. It is just as easy to turn your dwelling in a former cowshed or barn into a media hub as it is to work from a warehouse loft apartment. In the new electronic era, creating a working environment at home can be easy. Olivetti have a product that is as big as a floor cushion and houses all the necessities – CD-ROM drives, discs, mobile phone, calculator, and electronic diary with keyboard. The nomad just wraps it up in the protective quilt and carries it off to a new site.

Martha Stewart, American author of ten best-sellers and host of TV programmes on food, entertaining, gardening and home renovation, set up her office in the old mud-room, where boots and baskets

1 An artist's studio in a factory in Cadaqués in Spain is sensibly surfaced in white ceramics and warmed in winter with an old, ducted stove. Lightwells in between the rafters bring as much natural light into the painting area as possible.

2 Architects Peter Haverhals and Frank Heylen retained the workmanlike simplicity of this boarding school in Antwerp when they installed a monumental concrete-topped work-surface stretching the length of a classroom.

were once stored, in her home in Connecticut. An old farm table with a durable, galvanized aluminium top holds the docking station for her Apple PowerBook, her computer, printer and cellular phone. An overhead office shelving system is actually an antique pantry cabinet. The standard metal filing cabinets were spray-painted a porcelain green at an auto body shop, as was a steel-framed industrial tool cart on castors that carries the fax machine. Writing in her own highly successful magazine, *Martha Stewart Living*, she advises, 'Just as it is vital for children to have an area where they can write and study, we adults need a place of our own to work and think. It doesn't have to be a large space – the computer already permits us to consolidate greatly.'

Those with the good fortune to live on two – or even three – storeys can devote an entire floor to their work. Architect Miska

Miller and her husband Ross Lovegrove have a design practice on the ground floor of their concrete-and-steel 1950s warehouse in London. Their bedrooms and bathrooms are above the studio and they added another floor for living space which is 17m (55ft) long.

Australian food photographer Mark Chew and his wife Sally Ann Ballharrie, who live in a former hat factory in Melbourne, also combine their living space with their work area. Their photographic studio is on the ground floor, but for food photography

they need to use the kitchen, which is part of their first-floor open-plan living space. So that their entire residence did not become a work zone, they shielded the bed behind a freestanding wall that stops short of the rafters, and placed the kitchen on the other side.

A home office in a conventional residence often means squeezing cabinets and computer into a bedroom, garage, or kitchen corner. In factory and barn conversions, open-plan living leaves you free to carve out a work area or take over an entire floor. Converted space is all about flexibility.

Ice-cream Factory, NYC

A building as big as a city block

In New York, cosiness has never exerted the grip that it has on British popular taste. One of the reasons why loft living caught on in Manhattan long before it did in Milan and Munich is that New Yorkers value huge, untamed space which leaves exposed acres of cement, bare brick, boards as big as railway sleepers (ties) and joists that could span the Niagara Falls. Think big, and American loft-dwellers thought even bigger.

This triple-chimneyed former varnish (and later ice-cream) factory on the East River facing Manhattan is so large that the owners, Tim and Dagny Du Val, who inhabit one floor and have installed their landscape-garden business in one of the original furnace buildings, rent out spaces to a humidor-maker, a bakery, a coffee company, a sculptor, an artist, a wine-storage company and a gourmet-food purveyor.

Each furnace building is a single room with a hearth about 1.8m (6ft) deep, enclosed in an arched 1.8m (6ft) brick alcove. Three 13.7m (45ft)-high rectangular chimneys, connected along the width of the building, house the flues from the hearths, while the roofs of the furnace rooms are

supported by steel trusses that reach 6m (20ft) at their peaks.

Turning part of a factory that once produced toxic chemicals into a garden-design centre is in the spirit of the times. Garden plants growing over a former machine-age plant: an appropriate metaphor as American industry begins to think green. 'When we came here in 1982,' the owners recall, 'we took out about 920cu.m (1,200cu.yd) of garbage – even old trucks. We covered the building at once in Boston ivy, trained upon all of the chimneys.'

2

A run-down street-scape of blocks and warehouses, obsolete factories and chimneys, this gigantic complex bears a central portal dated 1850–1905. It was built to make varnishes in 1906. As is usual with varnish factories, there is an open central courtyard and this can be accessed by a walkway on the upper storey, or via the ground-floor entrance, used by trucks. Originally there were three structures here, the largest an L-shaped building, the second a complex of three furnace buildings, and the third (2) to the north, squaring off the ground plan. Additions over the years joined all these structures together.

Planning permission to convert the property was not a problem, but the zoning use was. 'In order to live on-site in an industrial zone, we had to apply as caretakers, but

that was appropriate with a landscape and plant business. Then justifying our presence to look after the plants was easy – in the event of a power failure, to water them, and to control heat in the greenhouse.' Fortunately, the Du Val's, had already renovated three lofts in New York so they were not daunted by the scale. But the solid construction posed an unusual problem. The building is so substantial that sinking a pool or a bath, or changing the windows, was impossible.

'Every time you try to make a hole you lose the drill,' the owners note. 'Everyone who works here ruins something. The biggest struggle was the plumbing, but we managed to run the pipes underneath the ceilings of the top floor.'

'New Yorkers value huge, untamed space . . . '

The Du Vals live on the top floor, in a part of the building that once housed an ice-cream factory. The main area measures an awesome 371sq.m (4,000sq.ft), the terrace it spills out onto (5) measures a further 325sq.m (3,500sq. ft) and the guest wing another 92sq.m (1,000sq.ft). The apartment and terrace overlook the city (3) across the East River towards mid-town Manhattan's East Side and the 59th Street (Queensboro) Bridge. The scale of the space is deceptive because of the ceiling heights. 'The floor-to-ceiling height is 4.8m (16ft), which makes the windows look small – in fact they are 240 x 90cm (8 x 3ft) which is pretty big.' To bring more light into the apartment, the Du Vals made several additional openings for windows in the structure, using jackhammers and then rebricking the holes. The original skylights – dating from the turn of the century when it was common to inset skylight openings all over industrial spaces – were left intact. Spots on track-lighting are hidden behind steel-cast, reinforced concrete beams; floor-mounted uplighters are moved depending on where they are needed.

The Du Vals' experience in converting other factories taught them to plan the open apartment around the central kitchen, keeping the bathroom and bedrooms as self-contained wings.

Construction work was limited to just one end, the east wing, to make these two bedrooms and bathrooms 'like cubes within that space – not like rooms boxing it in'. The vista of light from one end through to the other is important, as the space is open.

They also made a point of recycling what they found. Huge freezer doors, dating from the 1940s, lead to the bathroom; and one bathroom basin is an original ice-cream mixing bowl (6). Woodwork used to support the cooling pipes in a large ice-cream storage freezer has been recycled in the custom-built kitchen as kitchen counters (4). The floors are original terracotta tiles from the same era, with drainage in place from the days when they hosed the floor down. The walls are all bare brick, 30cm (1ft) thick. Most of the main walls had been covered with about twenty coats of paint. The owners ground them down until a little bit of each colour remained (1) – leaving a patina of different shades that acts as a unifying theme for the space, 'like old Pompeiian mosaics

LEADS TO TERRACES AND GUEST STUDIO WHERE PICTURES 2 & 3 WERE TAKEN

washed off'. When the walls
were cleaned, a green-blue
pigment emerged, which the
Du Vals replicated on the units
that support the worktops. The
cast-concrete ceiling is bare.

Furnishing is difficult with
rooms of this scale. Little pieces
do not work, which tends to rule
out bric-a-brac. The furniture
is not in a set layout, but is
movable for large parties.
Individual pieces date from many
periods: a square grand piano
from the 1860s, a pool table from
1906 and American bamboo
armchairs and sofas from the
1930s and 40s. 'We design terraces
throughout New York and so
are constantly creating that
feeling of inside blurred with
out. At night we look out on to
the floodlit garden.'

In the terrace garden, the pergola
has also been constructed from
old timbers salvaged from the
ice-cream freezers. The pool
and fountain are made from a
heavy old cog from a 1920s metal
foundry. Every growing thing
is planted in containers, foliage
spilling out over the sides so
that the pots are hidden. The
plants include quaking aspens,
birches, alpine and black pines,
all feathery and delicate with softly
coloured annuals mixed in. Many
of the specimens, orphans from
other schemes, have here been
pampered into health again.

4

Outdoor Spaces

Agricultural and industrial buildings both exclude the outside from the interiors. Industrial workplaces were never built to frame the view, and the high windows in old schoolhouses were deliberately placed so the view did not distract the pupils. Barns and tractor sheds never needed windows, and dairies deliberately excluded sunlight, in order to keep the interior cool. Creating an oasis of green in such a building can, therefore, be something of a challenge.

In inner-city conversions where light is blocked by tall buildings, new owners can sometimes create an inner courtyard either open to the sky, or beneath a glazed atrium. Architect Mark Guard's conversion of a garage in south London, for example, surrounds a central open

space planted with slender, silvery *Betula jacquemontii* trees growing through granite chips.

Herbaceous flowerbeds and manicured lawns suit neither the agricultural nor the city workplace conversion. These are more suited to a minimal, Japanese style, like that of Guard's courtyard arranged with pebbles and gravel. Or they may continue brick or stone flooring from the interior, softened by containers planted with bamboo, box or bay. A planting plan may be as simple as stacking containers of flowers down a cast-iron fire escape,

① Australian architect Ray Gill established the garden area first when he began his conversion of a spring factory. This lush courtyard is designed to be very low maintenance, and leads to the guest quarters, with a loft sleeping area.

② The ground floor of a converted boarding school in Antwerp, designed by architect Hugo Kinnear, makes the most of a view through floor-to-ceiling windows.

③ Glenn Murcutt's aerodynamically shaped makeover of an old tractor shed looks out over indigenous Australian foliage of eucalyptus and tallow wood.

1 The top floor of a converted Antwerp school was designed by owners Ronald Merens and Betty Bergen. The elegant lines of clipped shrubs are a perfect solution for the neat inner courtyard.

2 Mark Guard's converted garages in Deptford, south London, have a Japanese-style courtyard with slender, silvery trees. Its minimalist lines echo those of the spare interior.

3 In Melbourne's favourable climate a courtyard becomes an outdoor living space. Architect Michael Rigg emphasized this Victorian foundry's grand proportions by using low-key, square-cut hedges.

but as many loft apartments include terraces or roof gardens, more ambitious schemes are possible. Before embarking upon any design, however simple, check that your terrace or roof is load-bearing.

If you opt for a garden without containers you will need to decide what the plants will grow in – Grow-bags or a fibrous soil replacement – as well as how they will be watered – with a simple watering can or a specially designed irrigation system. London-based gardener Dan Pearson created a garden without soil, especially for loft-dwellers, at the Chelsea Flower Show in 1996. He used a pioneering German-made fibre called GroDan, which is as thick and light as loft insulation and only requires a sprinkling of fertilizer and water to support good ground cover like thyme and lavender, sage and fennel, santolina and purple thrift.

The wind can be a problem on sky-high terraces, so rather than put up windbreaks of climber-covered trellises, choose plants that do not mind exposed sites. Flexible tall grasses make a feature of the wind, and silver-foliaged Mediterranean plants thrive in positions with little shade and can withstand very dry conditions.

Covering a hard surface with soft foliage and interesting plants that move in the wind creates a meditative space, so treat the garden area as an extra room and move in some furniture. This does not have to be the standard wooden benches or traditional cast-iron chairs and tables: British architects Jonathan McDowell and Renato Benedetti designed rooftop seating from toughened glass that reflects the light from the River Thames, which slides below their conversion in a former tea warehouse.

5

In making the structural changes to your conversion, you have worn three hats, as owner, designer and builder. No matter how many people you have employed as stand-ins for the latter two roles, at last the time will come for you to make the final choices on how to furnish the space. Settle back and watch how the light falls on the walls of your home. Work out what will bring comfort and colour, as well as amusement and practicality, to your environment.

Industrial and agricultural buildings have an architectural integrity that defies camouflage behind traditional decoration such as repeat patterns on papers, fabrics and wall-to-wall floor coverings. But austerity is not the only choice. Colour on walls, ceilings and floors can help to soften them visually, make spatial divisions or unify a scheme. Differences in textures help to reinforce these divisions: for example, tiled floors and walls in the kitchen, and plaster or wood in a living area. Soft furnishings bring comfort to hard surfaces. Bare brick, tinted glass, wooden boards and steel joists contrast with the more sensuous materials like paper panels, wool throws, linen slipcovers, canvas screens, hessian (burlap) drapes and silk cushions.

Recycled industrial furnishings from hospitals, architectural salvage yards or army-surplus stores, junk-shop finds, antiques and cutting-edge contemporary designs look equally at home in a renovated barn or factory. Furniture on castors makes the choice of, say, a chair for general seating, dining or watching television a flexible one, governed by whim or simply by the changing light.

The single most important thing to remember when furnishing a conversion is not to let the architectural scale dwarf your possessions. Think big, and free up floor space by storing clutter. Relaxing, sleeping, bathing, cooking, eating – tick off the areas in your space that need special storage requirements. There are never enough drawers or cupboards, and you can look for unconventional ways of storing things in your unconventional space.

Then look to the smaller elements: 'God is in the details,' as Mies van der Rohe said. Without period detailing like cornices, mouldings and architraves, let alone doors, attention focuses on the smaller elements – taps, banisters and light fixtures, as well as on the way you hang pictures or group furniture. When architectural details exist, or industrial fittings remain, they can be highlighted in the overall design.

Furnishing and decorating decisions are not irrevocable. After adding colour you can always return to neutrals, after choosing plains you can introduce pattern, after minimizing possessions you can still bring home a classic chair from a second-hand office supplier. So now is the time to put the white wine into a fireman's bucket to chill for your house-warming.

1 Colour can play a part in defining a space or simply introducing a new element to a room. In the deliberately dark entrance hall in this barn conversion on the north Norfolk coast, the undulating staircase wall was painted a sea-green and leads up to the light-flooded building above.

2 Another vital element in furnishing at this stage is storage, which can be as flexible as trolleys or as permanent as these custom-built units that act as partition walls.

5 Colour

Design Elements

'I love colours when they don't exist too much. Life always comes with its own colour; your friends, flowers, things. So you don't have to have so much of it in your decor,' comments Andrée Putman, who comes out in support of mono-chrome rooms as a background for colourful living. A neutral frame-work is just one of many options for manipulating colour. In an open-plan space, colour can be used to divide or to unify areas. If, as psychotherapists believe, our response to colour is emotional (pink, for example, is calming and red invigorating), you will either have a flamboyant urge to colour-in bold backgrounds, or you may prefer to show restraint and let the natural shades of wood and stone, brick and plaster colour the interior.

The orientation of your space can affect the use of colour in an open-plan environment: natural light that pours in through a window-wall or skylight will soften bright colours and make an all-white space brighter, while shadows on a wall will change the feel of a colour altogether.

Bold colours can be overwhelming on large surface areas, so coloured partition walls or screens acting as accent colours are visually more manageable. Besides, without rooms, colours in open spaces will affect each other. So before launching into intense, contrasting colour schemes on big surfaces, think about the way the surroundings will determine the final result: a yellow square framed in white will appear smaller than an identical square framed in black, and a black frame, unlike a white frame, will appear to be in the foreground. Tone also changes, so yellow on a white background appears more lemon than on a black background.

Colours can change the dimensions of a space, so using a lot of colour

The pale palette can be interesting if it accompanies an austere minimalism and some fine-lined furniture.

1 In the absence of strong colour, try to emphasize architectural features such as these double doors.

2 White walls, white curtains and a white platform support this white linen bed. The sculptural shape of a dark, wood canoe from Thailand, which runs the length of the wall in Bob Callender and Liz Ogilvie's converted cinema in Scotland, makes a contrasting addition to a monochrome room.

1 A church conversion in South Africa shows how a high-ceilinged space with gothic doors can take strong colour. Artist Beazy Bailey painted the bare brick indigo, framed the woodwork in aquamarine and chose crimson, full-length curtains to match the concertinaed ceiling.

2 Splashes of red introduced by the poster and the upholstered modern chair lend glamour to the bare cement floors in this white-painted, converted 1920s warehouse in Melbourne, Australia.

compensates for a sparser, more edited furnishing scheme. Warm tones like red, orange or yellow will bring a surface visually closer, while sharper, contrasting accent colours will heighten or lighten the effect. In the absence of period detailing, like cornices and mouldings, accent colours in hard-edged open-spaced conversions are often introduced through furnishings. The combination of colours, together with the lighting and size of the space, will determine the overall feeling, whether bold or subdued, coolly contemporary or richly decorative.

A broad swatch of paint across a surface will help you to see how the colour looks when the daylight falls upon it and how it changes under electric light, which intensifies strong colours. Surfaces and materials will influence your choice of paint colour. Bare brick or plaster walls, tongue-and-groove panelling, or floorboards all absorb and reflect surface colour differently. Consider all the surfaces: walls, ceilings, floors and doors. 'Never determine colours for big surfaces in big, open spaces too early,' is the cautionary advice from Ken Charles, who converted a 1940s veterinary-supply factory in Melbourne. He ended up letting natural materials colour the space – glass with a green edge to it, sandstone on the floor, unplastered, mellowed brick-work and woodwork in white.

Urban loft-dwellers often favour big, open, white spaces with splashes of colour in the forms of a sofa, rug or painting. A neutral background allows more control of colour in a converted space, where details become focal points. In the design of an all-white, open-plan living area in a schoolhouse conversion, the only colour accents allowed by architect Brian Ma Siy are found in the lampshades made of Murano glass. Moved about the space, they add peripatetic accents of colour.

Part of the fun of an industrial conversion is the freedom to use swathes of strong colour on the walls that the average room in a purpose-built home cannot take. An existing wall can be painted either to show spatial divisions between a living area and an adjoining dining area or to separate an upstairs gallery area from a ground floor. In such cases the

colour on the wall can be extended up to the height of the imaginary ceiling. Painted walls can highlight a stairwell or entrance area to make a spatial distinction. Self-assured artists can paint their walls orange and fuchsia in horizontal and vertical planes like abstract paintings. Artist Andrew Logan and architect Michael Davis heightened the walls in their 1950s garage and then painted them the colour of blood oranges, with two wide doorways framed in Yves Klein blue. Beneath the glazed roof, sunlight bathes these vibrant walls in dazzling light.

Floors can be coloured by painting them or covering them with rugs and carpets. Unless the floorboards need replacing, consider painting those in high traffic areas with a high gloss paint, grouting any gaps between them in a contrasting colour and, like designer Ross Lovegrove and Miska Miller, filling nail-stud holes with a heavy-duty car-body filler also in a contrasting colour. Floor coverings can suggest boundaries and define seating and eating areas. A bright rug in a living area becomes a simple focal point around which sofas and chairs can be grouped.

1 Vibrant blue in a converted bank brings the walls back from decorative obscurity.

▶ *Clockwise from top left*: terracotta in a Toronto factory; indigo framing a porthole window; shocking pink and purple; blue accents echo the main theme; an orange kitchen screen; bright yellow walls with a galleried floor in mint.

Applying colour, then softening it by rag-rubbing or scumbling, brings the patina of age to newly plastered walls.

1 The sultry purple wall in the bathroom of Laurence Kriegel's loft is emphasized by the gleaming brass plumbing, a pristine white basin and a bulkhead light.

2 Instant theatricality was achieved in a converted seed warehouse in San Antonio, Texas, by rubbing lavender and ochre into the wash on the huge pillar and accenting the subtle colour by painting a slender column purple.

In rural conversions colour tends to be used more naturally. Everyone in the local village store in Lenox, Massachusetts, recalls the new owners of a converted carriage barn, Rodney Ripps and Helen Verin, handing over a jar of butternut-squash soup to ask for that exact colour in paint. Now their large kitchen walls are painted in this distinctive colour, with the wood trims and original cross-braced stable door accented in the colour of curry powder. In striking contrast to the living spaces, their home office is 'the colour of beetroot'.

Let the colours in the landscape – or townscape – inspire your paint choice. Lifestyle magazine publisher Martha Stewart's brand of paints in the United States was inspired by the Araucana and Ameraucana chickens she keeps. These oil-based shades for country dwellers are made in the soft colour of eggs – from whites and browns to turquoise and olive. Ralph Lauren's paint colours inspired by Madison County are earthy naturals, while

his metallic range for metropolitan living has the industrial gleam of the automobile industry.

Whether you want to leave strong colour to the accessories or try out something bold on a big surface, the easiest way to decide how keen you are on a colour is to experiment with shades on a moveable item before painting the big picture. Rugs can be moved around, banners replaced, throws and screens changed. Try out hot orange and lime green, or choose different shades from the pale palette to find out how much colour you can take and whether you prefer most of the colour to come from the background or the furnishings. Colour on large surfaces should be the last decision you make, as it is the one that determines the immediate atmosphere of your converted space.

5 Texture

Design Elements

Textures on walls, floors and furnishings can make a space feel hard or soft, warm or cold; they can affect the way light is reflected or absorbed and how sound will reverberate. Used in combination with colour, or to vary a monochrome scheme, texture goes further than merely visible surface treatment to create a tactile impression in your home environment. The unclad building materials of a factory or barn – stone, brick, concrete, plaster, wood – introduce interior textures that are different from the plastered finishes found in a traditional house. Leaving these hard-edged surfaces unclad lets the space retain its industrial feel. Any new surface treatments that affect the structure should respond to the architecture, which is why frosted glass blocks make such a

good material for partitioning within smooth concrete or brick walls. This hard, industrial surfacing can then be softened by adding textiles to walls, windows and floors.

The integrity of the materials is important in any conversion, even if the contemporary solution breaks with the vernacular architecture. Wooden or stone agricultural interiors can be clad in smooth steel panelling or corrugated iron, with heavy fabrics to balance the weight of the building material. In a timber-framed Essex cottage with whitewashed wattle-and-daub walls, minimalist architect John Pawson added

1 A change of texture can define proportions. White-painted reinforced-steel joists extend to ceiling height, while roughened, bare brick walls above the domestic living space, panelled with white-painted partition board, are highlighted with uplighters.

2 A converted chemical labotatory in Belgium is given a grass-green carpet on the cork floor. The wooden rectangular plinth that anchors one corner is balanced by the dark, painted column in another.

3 In a monochrome scheme it is the difference in texture between white-painted wood, white linen blinds and whitewashed walls that makes the space interesting. A woven mat and a log basket on the pale beech floor introduce still more textures, and a sepia ink wash on the framed canvas hung above the door is a decorator's trick to take the eye upwards.

1 Blue accents in an anonymous white-walled, wooden-floored space create an interesting room set. Tartan-upholstered dining chairs are contrasted with a yellow plaid.

2 In a converted barn in Normandy, owner Julie Prisca emphasizes the tongue-and-groove aqua walls by changing the direction of the stripe on the yellow café curtain. Beyond, in the living area, she has hung an Eastern textile on a bare brick wall.

low, white-plastered screens to create divisions that harmonize with the original fabric of the building. Instead of laying flagstones, he mixed pigments into concrete for a silvery, fluid-looking floor. Uninterrupted by slabs, it is the perfect foil for both the intricate geometry of the original timber-and-lathe structure and the smooth, white screens later introduced, and the texture is similar to the vernacular stone.

Interior designer John Stefanidis illustrates the importance of getting the right feel for new materials in his conversion of a dairy. Mud and straw originally littered the earth floors. To make it habitable, Stefanidis chose brick flooring, believing that the nearest equivalent to clay – terracotta tiles – would have introduced a Mediterranean feel that would have been wholly inappropriate. He also considered wood, but this would have had the wrong sound when walked upon.

One way to achieve an appropriately aged texture is to use reclaimed materials. In Australia the architect

Glenn Murcutt sought recycled timbers for the walls and floors of a converted tractor shed built of tallow wood – which still grows on the property – because the width of boards made from mature trees matched the age of the rustic barn.

When Miska Miller and Ross Lovegrove converted their 1950s warehouse in London into a studio and family living space, they tried out a number of different materials within their white-walled, wooden-floored, open-plan apartment. The original small windows were enhanced with strip lights set into the galvanized steel frame. Aircraft flooring in honeycombed fibreglass, a material that innovative designers like for its tensile strength and lightness, was used for the kitchen units and bath panels. A banquet-sized wooden dining table designed by Ross is supported by four steel columns at each corner, which double as uplighters. Their sink is moulded in carbon fibre.

Creating different textures can be as simple as changing the method of paint application – spray-gunning paint onto plastered walls, the way that automobile factories do, burnishes them like lacquer, while hand-painting or using rags and sponges creates a more rustic effect. Alternatively, change the pattern and weave of fabrics on furnishings. In

generously proportioned open spaces you will have to be cautious about introducing too much pattern. Unlined hessian (burlap) or canvas drapes can replace conventional curtains, and the weighty quality complements a hard, industrial interior. Sometimes a complete change can be fun. Joseph Corré and Serena Rees broke out of anonymity in their London loft with giant, multi-coloured swirling spots – like polka dots – on their floor-to-ceiling curtains designed

by Joseph's mother, fashion designer Vivienne Westwood. Westwood also designed a leopard-skin duvet cover which sprawls on their padded black bed. Sensuous soft furnishings were also sought by Ross Lovegrove and Miska Miller, who concealed their stacking boxes for clothes behind pairs of pewter and gold coloured curtains made of soft rubber, another material inspired by industry.

When, in the 1920s, London's fashionable drawing rooms were drained of colour under the direction of interior designer Syrie Maugham, Cecil Beaton recalled the importance of textures in bringing vitality and interest to the all-white room: 'glass fibre, sheets of gelatine, cutlet frills, coils of carnival paper streamers, doves, egg boxes, cardboard plates, plaster carvings, driftwood branches.' This illustrates how mainstream decoration filters down into spontaneous and frivolous interpretations. Now that you have all the hard surfaces worked out, introduce some recycled textures for the accessories.

◀ *Clockwise from top left*: cut-outs doors by designer Ross Lovegrove; patterned acid-etched glass is echoed in a mesh chair; old rafters in a barn conversion by William Leddy reveal the building's origins and are juxtaposed with new steel joists; a polished cement floor forms the background to a rounded wooden partition.

1️⃣ An in-built steel fireplace framed by a contrasting concrete slab adds to the different layers of texture in this contemporary interior.

5

Furniture

Design Elements

The old formality that rooms imposed upon furniture arrangements has gone, along with the rigid and hierarchical sense of order that accompanied it. In a converted space, furniture is mobile, casual and flexible. Pairs of chairs or sofas on either side of the hearth, a desk at the window, the head of the table signified by the carver chair, the 'master' bedroom with connecting bathroom are furniture configurations that are relegated to the past. Decorators have had to learn to furnish without a room plan and, as a result, wide-open spaces are now furnished with informal, fluid arrangements. Flexibility suits a more casual way of life. There are several furnishing routes to choose from, but keep in mind your preferences for colour and texture. Remember, too, that furnishings can be diminished by awesome floor-to-ceiling heights. Custom-made built-ins that are designed to make the most of grand spaces are the most expensive and inflexible option; pieces sourced in salvage yards and second-hand shops are the least expensive. Or you could be swept up in the cutting-edge style of loft-living and go for the latest designer chair or classic pieces of modern furniture.

Frank Lloyd Wright crustily observed that 'human beings must group, sit or recline, confound them, and they must dine', so rather than permit his clients to

move into his stylish prairie-style houses and fill all that horizontal space with living-room suites in shiny velour and walnut veneer, he set about designing built-in furniture that reflected the style of the architecture. Lutyens did the same, scaling his cumbersome Edwardian benches, sofas and console tables to the right proportions for the imposing rooms. Architectonic, built-in furniture has returned with pieces designed to match the scale of industrial spaces and to define boundaries. In their open-plan, windowless warehouse in London, Jan Kaplicky and Amanda Levete have a low, curving MDF wall that doubles as furniture and as a partition, standing two-thirds of the height of the party walls. Wrapping

Not all loft conversions use modern designer-furniture, but all have an interest in unusual furniture collections.

1 In Craig Port's Cape Town warehouse conversion, junk-shop 1930s furniture and a Le Corbusier chaise-longue resolve their differences.

2 *Faux animaux* leopard and tiger skin, a leather Chesterfield, and a zebra skin create a baroque interior in a converted schoolhouse belonging to a video producer. All is retro – the pendant light is the modern design icon for Flos by Achille Castiglione.

3 Plain white sheeting upholsters junk-shop wing armchairs in stylist Sue Skeen's London warehouse. Furniture is accessorized with white wood and steel.

around the bathroom and the kitchen like a screen, it ends up as a circular bed. Rather than having sofas and chairs, Kaplicky and Levete built a central platform in their open living area and set a niche in it for the television; upholstered, organic shapes set into the platform can be used for curling up on.

The alternative to built-in furniture is furniture that stacks, folds or moves about on industrial castors. In big open spaces it is useful to have a flexible furnishing scheme for when friends drop in; or if you wish to move your seating to follow the last of the evening sun; or because more workspace is needed in, say, the kitchen. After all, you can push around a chair, or even a filing cabinet on castors, as easily as a vacuum cleaner, and stacking or folding furniture that can be pulled up to a dining table in an instant does not stand around waiting for the party to begin.

Patient sleuthwork in architectural salvage yards and auctions can be highly rewarding, often producing inexpensive and large-scale pieces. Rejects from old hospitals, like lockers, washstands and truckle (trundle) beds on wheels, can furnish a bed and bathing space. Cylindrical radiators, old school washstands, and office furniture from the 1950s also adapt to domestic use with surprising ease. Other unlikely sources throw up all kinds of usable objects. Yacht

chandlers' stock cleats and halyards will double as stair rigging, while hammocks stretch between rafters. Art suppliers have a choice of strong papers, files and boxes; army-surplus stores sell metal storage boxes and army blankets for sofa throws; and professional caterers have steel trolleys, rails and pails. Turn an old loading-bay door with its iron cross-bracing into a table on trestle legs and buy 12 stacking or folding chairs. Put an old store cupboard on industrial castors and wheel it next to the oven. Insulate the walls with paperback books on metal shelving, and buy airport stairs to access the library. Orange crates stacked for pantry storage, or a test-tube rack doubling as a spice rack would look out of place in a conventional household, but a converted space presents endless opportunities for recycling industrial design to make your domestic life more interesting.

① Ross Lovegrove designed both these yellow stacking chairs and the table legs that double as uplighters for use in his own home – a radical, remodelled 1950s warehouse in London.

② MDF storage units, built on an enamel frame set on rollers, can be pulled into place for instant screening in this warehouse conversion.

③ Deep grooves for underfloor cabling were glassed over in a converted power station in Texas. The furniture, all set on industrial rollers, looks unnervingly as though it runs along these tracks.

④ The industrial undercarriage on a dining-room table enables it to move into any position.

1 Uncluttered white space with simple wooden, white or monochrome articles is the choice of New York interior designer Vicente Wolf for his apartment in a former clothes manufacturing factory. The floors are concrete painted white and etched in squares like tiles. On this high-gloss surface, the gilded black Directoire chair and the low Indonesian table create a little still life with the photographs that Wolf props against the walls.

2 The light in this New York loft encouraged the owner to use Italian glass from different periods. A table by Philippe Starck for Fiam, a vase and stool by Gaetano Pesce and a lamp in Murano glass from Venini bring a splash of colour.

3 In a newly converted industrial space, an old period piece can bring character, like this ballfoot leather armchair standing next to a modern magazine table and white sofa on wheels.

Mixtures of contemporary and traditional furniture work best if they are on the right scale. Massive couches with scrolled arms and claw feet, cabinets with block bases and marble-topped chests can hold their own against awesome volumes and industrial surfaces better than antiques from a more delicate age. Nevertheless, second-hand shops can turn up traditional pieces – like Biedermeier or Directoire, both scaled for a more spacious era – that will not be over-whelmed in an imposing open space. New York interior designer Vicente Wolf furnished his own 185sq.m (2,000sq.ft) apartment in an old clothes manufacturing factory in mid-town Manhattan with a collection of antiques set against a monochrome palette. The walls – still bearing the holes where the sewing machines were once bolted

– are painted white, and the concrete floors are whitened with glossy shipdeck paint. In this pristine, all-white modernist box, small groups of gilt and rococo chairs, a French 1940s pickled-and-limed-oak cabinet, and low Rajasthani bronze-and-wood tables are boldly juxtaposed with Thai sculptures, crucifixes from all over the world, a black-and-white photographic collection and an original Raoul Dufy.

Behind the imposing façade of Carol and Philip Thomas's 'palazzo', classic furnishings are grouped on a palatial scale. Although their *faux* marbled floor is linoleum, Carol mixes antiques, brocades and silks against the cement walls and then accents that richness with unlined hessian (burlap) drapes at the windows.

The kitchen is equipped with 1950s industrial-sized American appliances and illuminated by a French chandelier.

Stylish interiors are always planned around contrasts. Architect Glenn Murcutt highlighted the contemporary conversion of an old tractor shed by furnishing the entire single-roomed studio with modern classics: Arne Jacobsen's 'Ant' chair shares space with beds by Alvar Aalto and chairs by Le Corbusier. Artist's agent Antonia Polizzi lives in a former paint warehouse in which architect John Beckmann let graceful but heavy iron pillars interrupt the open plan. The pillars support a wall of frosted-glass slats, which forms the backdrop for a juxtaposition of antiques with Memphis modern, mostly in black and white, reflecting the owner's graphic sensibilities.

Furniture often reveals individual enthusiasms which is why, in the adventurous conversions of former workplaces, you find so many twentieth-century design classics alongside contemporary designer labels. Only a few functional pieces are needed to start the collection. Architect Brian Ma Siy's huge, steel-topped table is the centre of family life, the place where his son does his homework, where the family prepares food, cooks and dines. Old or new, recycled or tailor-made, the best furnishings are those that reflect the inhabitant's life-style, and are used with imagination.

Design Elements

In the past, when each room was dedicated to a specific function, arranging the details was as easy as bussing in a load of props. A painting, pretty china, a few books, an obelisk and something ethnic from travels abroad – you can recognize the ubiquitous accessories from every photographed location. These gestures to lighten and brighten an interior define your attitude, and can make your routine easier, too. They can be as major as surgery or as transient as flowers.

Detail can define the success of two apartments in the same block: one, an open, white space with views out over the rooftops of the city, is exhilarating; the other, with a dim, inner core, is a bit claustrophobic. Imagine these two different schemes to appreciate just how important these final flourishes are: in the first, plain, white walls draw the onlooker towards the open windows where there are

comfortable club chairs clustered around tables. Metallic-shaded, tall lamps beam down light where it is needed, while overhead uplighters on a steel beams cast light upwards for a softer overall effect. Sweet-scented plants grow in little silver buckets; white roses and lilies in glass vases are dotted about the space out of the way of traffic. In the other apartment, a forlorn sofa stands across the run of windows, the table lamps dotted about the empty space have to be switched on individually, so many of them have not been lit and – there is nothing as ghostly as white lampshades without illumination. Whatever the dimensions of the space, it is the arrangement of the furnishings and lighting that encourages people to feel comfortable, or makes them feel lost or unwelcome.

Converted spaces may retain architectural or structural references to their industrial past, as generic as steel supporting columns and exposed ceiling beams or as unusual as a copper vat once used for storing hops, or rings that once held horses' hay bags. These industrial heirlooms provide more character than purpose-built homes could ever hope to achieve. More sophisticated architectural details like cornices and mouldings will probably be lacking unless the building is a neoclassical one such as an old bank, but this does not mean they cannot be added.

1 A copy of a large-scale design by Ross Lovegrove is an interesting backdrop to his friendly chairs and Noguchi lanterns.

2 Letraset sheets, postcards, Polaroids and news cuttings in a steel frame form a theatrical device that takes the eye upwards.

3 The great shell of an abandoned shoe factory owned by artist and glass designer Marie Ducate is brightened and prettified by an eclectic mix of furniture from different decades.

A pediment on a freestanding partition wall makes a clever postmodern statement – as well as a frame for a collection of paintings – and wainscoting and moulding in an enclosed area such as a bathroom add definition within the open space.

Other details might emerge as you go about adapting an interior. Shadow gaps are a modern detail favoured by architects if you plan to plaster the party walls. A fine, deep line etched into plaster 6mm ($^1/_4$ in) above where the floorboards meet the walls makes the boards appear to slip away inside the wall. Alternatively, a slender floor-to-ceiling door to the bathroom that clicks shut as smoothly and silently as an expensive car door, or a spiral staircase in the centre of a floor plan, which divides the space and leads the eye towards a gallery above, provide structural details that refine an expansive space. Fewer doors, walls and openings mean that each transition can be special. In a converted space, because there are no standard number of rooms, as there are in the average brick or wooden house, you don't have to buy a set of standardized, panelled doors. Instead, you can invest in a single, monumental, custom-built one on superior hinges with a single chrome handle styled to fit into the hand as smoothly as worry beads.

Successful arrangements need focal points, which is decorator-speak for the positions that attract most attention. They are as easy to create

as propping pictures against white walls, or giving a single unusual object a conspicuous setting. When he was penniless in the 1960s, American designer Vicente Wolf waited at an architectural salvage company for hours, in the cold, in order to buy a 1920s French, green marble fireplace surround. Only when he got home did he remember that he did not have a fireplace. Now it is at the centre of his collection of black-and-white photographs, which he props on the mantelpiece. An Irvin Penn image of a flower sits on the hearth like a fireguard. Other details maintain the black-and-white

theme. Flowers in the house are always white: tube roses in Eastern pots and white day lilies in tall, glass cylinders standing on the white deck floor. At the floor-to-ceiling grid of steel-framed windows, white blinds glide from the floor upwards to stop at the height of a sofa, and a leafy indoor tree adds a spot of colour, while filtering the light.

While industrial conversions remain refreshingly free of sentiment, though not always of kitsch, the same cannot be said of renovations in the countryside, where a prolifer-ation of rush-and-willow baskets, old hay forks, saddles and harnesses, weathervanes and lanterns can make dwellings look like a theme park. Country crafts need careful editing to accessorize the place. One success story is that of two Californian collectors of antique Americana and folk art, who furnished their barn in New England to become a showcase for their well-honed collec-tion. Within the open-plan space there are wooden bowls, measures, mills and grinders, blanket chests, wing chairs covered in Ralph Lauren fabric, rag rugs and stags' antlers, as well as fine chairs and benches with a certain Puritan functionalism. Each piece is carefully arranged to highlight the quality of the object rather than the quantity in the collection.

Not all of us are collectors of fine antiques or contemporary design,

but details can be effective just by being simple and well placed. Terence Conran's advice that 'plain simple things are superior to flashy, complicated ones', holds true as much for a door handle as for a sofa. From taps to cup-board-door handles, stair rails to storage systems, details personalize your space and translate individual character into design. The finishing touches to an apartment in a converted building are crucial to the trans-formation of an inhospitable and obsolete former workplace into a welcoming contemporary home.

1 The theatrical column introduces a neoclassical touch to a large monochrome box. A thoroughly contemporary collection of black-and-white photographs is a backdrop to steel-and-leather Eileen Gray 1920s chairs.

▶ *Spiral from top left*: details make doors, stairs and landings distinctive. Door handles created from tubular rods are inset in a metal grasp; a template rectangle cut out of a door interlocks with the opposing surround; MDF grasp circles stuck onto a grey door give the same effect as rubber-stud flooring; cables strung out between steel clasps joined with pegs function as banisters – an idea taken from yacht rigging; ancient and modern are contrasted in a barn conversion, whose wooden structure has been cut away to reveal colourful wiring; light switches can ruin the uninterrupted flow of wall space – banking them in this chrome panel tidies them up; an image of how time passes in a sur-real set-up by Vicente Wolf; glass panels bolted to the stair landings add a touch of sophistication beside a black reinforced-steel joist; studs in stair treads are grouted with car-body filler in different colours, while the stairs are panelled in yellow acrylic.

6

An Old Barn, Normandy

A painterly, pale palette

Every year thousands of barns become derelict or are pulled down. Since barns are usually planned to relate to other farm buildings and to orientate to the sun, preservationists agree that, wherever possible, they should remain on their original sites, in their vernacular context. The Russian-born artist Yuri Kuper's renovation and extension of a Normandy barn at Mont Chatou, a large seventeenth-century estate, set amid the apple orchards and lush pastures typical of the region, is as much a testament to the skill of the builders 300 years ago as to the bold decision-making of the new owner, and proves that it is often better to adapt and transform than to demolish.

In his paintings, Yuri Kuper 'enfolds everyday objects in poetic meditation', as Peter Selz observed in the Pushkin Museum catalogue to Kuper's 1995 exhibition. Inkwells holding a single clover, old newsprint, letter flaps, empty picture frames, boxes, plates, brushes and scraps of paper layered upon pewtered backgrounds – all these hint at creativity on many levels, talent and good fortune. The colours are subdued, the message ambivalent. Something old, something new. Painter, sculptor and print-maker, Yuri Kuper 'perceives provocative shapes,

2

surfaces and tones in the discarded refuse of our disposable era' as Robert Flynn Johnson writes. So when the artist bought the deserted barn in Normandy, he sought to keep the spirit – and the structure – of the original building in its conversion to a studio home.

The wooden-framed barn, filled in with clay from the local potteries, had been well protected by its slate roof. Yuri Kuper bought a second barn and with the help of Jacques Marc, an architect who specializes in the salvage of old wood-framed structures, dismantled it and used it to extend both ends of the studio, creating a new entrance to the north (2) and a galleried bedroom beneath the eaves to the south (1). To benefit from the south-facing aspect, he added a large window (5) to the main barn. On the west, they used the remaining roughly cut beams to build a simple verandah, which he calls Eiffel, after the slender columns that support the rafters. Now he has an alfresco

dining room that is sheltered from the rain. As he says, 'Normandy has sudden showers, yet this space has that summery feeling of being outside but protected.'

Central to the configuration of the space is the core of the double-height barn which, acting as a conduit for light, is an ideal place in which to paint (3). Yet 'it doesn't look like an artist's studio or a living room', Kuper says. 'It's a very special open space where it is easy to paint.' He has kept the interior palette pale, but interesting, by rubbing grey and white into the wood of the timber frame, the stairs and the furniture. The salvaged staircase which leads to his bedroom was scumbled with layers of white acrylic, which in turn were sanded down between coats to achieve a silvery patina. Wood whitened like driftwood, and the smooth whitewashed clay walls, make the monochrome room a highly textured one.

Robert Flynn Johnson writes that 'through the alchemy of art', Yuri Kuper 'transforms, reshapes and reintroduces colours, textures, forms that would otherwise be invisible to our impatient consciousness'. Yuri Kuper confesses that he sees himself as a 'professional magician of surface – each has particular qualities that invite meditation'. He wanted to create a hazy and indefinite layered background. 'I am only a means of

looking, a way of seeing and a way of making people see,' he says.

Like porcelain, the clay walls of the barn are light-reflective, and after space, light is the most important element in the central studio, home to Kuper's canvases, easels and paint materials. Six skylights were cut into the roof, and he awakes to the tapping of branches on the windowpanes overhead. At night, a multitude of swivelling spotlights allow changes in the direction of the light.

Throughout the renovation Yuri Kuper chose what he called 'poor materials' – salvaged wood, roughly cut timbers, original wooden planks for the floors in the living area, and hardwood railway sleepers (ties)

for the verandah floor. In the rural setting he has chosen to furnish his barn with industrial pieces: solid old door chests, a large enamelled cast-iron wood-burning stove from Sweden for the studio, and factory furniture adapted into vanity units or chests-of-drawers. 'Everything has a subdued appearance, like it is hiding inside the walls.'

PLAN: Arrows in blue denote upper level
View of main entrance (2) not shown on plan

Carpenters' workbenches, old architectural plan chests and type-cases from the days of hot-metal printing furnish his studio (3, 6). Just as the barn builder took pride in his tools and wielded them with great skill, Yuri Kuper, who often paints brushes and inkwells, is fascinated by the tools with which craftsmen cut, chisel, hew and drill. A collection of craftsmen's tools form a still life on narrow

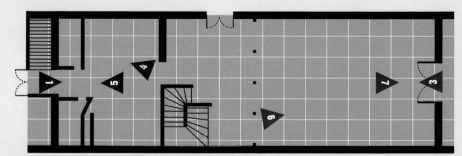

MAIN ENTRANCE

203

shelves lining the walls. 'I have a great respect for artisans' work,' he says. 'Today everybody writes manifestos but they cannot draw two lines.' Technical drawings he found in Paris also testify to the skills of the artisan.

Yuri Kuper's favourite room is the ground-floor kitchen, with its double doors topped by a semicircular glazed fanlight to allow extra light. Simply furnished with an old farmhouse table, corner cupboards and garden benches, and the *objets trouvés* that he picks up in his trawls of junk shops, it is designed, he says, 'to dissolve itself into nature.' Scrubbed, sanded, scoured, swabbed to near colourlessness, the barn is shaped, like driftwood, by sand, sun and water and the will of the artist. The gentle austerity of the place has a timelessness that embraces both past and future.

5 Storage

Design Elements

It is true that the more space people have, the less they want to hand over to storage. Jane and John Pinnington, who own a modest 93sq.m (1,000sq.ft) apartment in a former chemical storage warehouse in Liverpool, England, worked out that a typical suburban three-bedroom house of the same size would actually have more storage space. Perhaps it is an aversion to doors that prevents people from planning a line-up of useful cupboards. Perhaps built-in closets are avoided because unusually high ceilings make it impossible to use stock doors, and custom-made ones are expensive. But storage does not have to be behind closed doors. The solution could be as simple as taking a section of a room, running a rail through it, and hanging floor-to-ceiling curtains to create a walk-in dressing area.

Improvisation will create space, but careful planning within will make it functional. Specialist storage shops feature a selection of Shaker boxes, cardboard organizers and pigeonhole stack systems that can be arranged and installed within larger units to maintain the clean lines of the space, or left exposed.

It is unusual to find conventional storage like armoires and closets, dressers and sideboards, vanity units and chests of drawers scattered around open-plan apartments. They look awkward if they are not large enough to

Storage does not have to be permanent: it can be adjustable shelving, or can move about on wheels or stack in boxes.

1 His and hers clothing cupboards are concealed behind soft rubber curtaining in the home of designer Ross Lovegrove and his wife Miska Miller.

2 An old meat-safe cupboard, given a glass panel in place of its original wire-mesh front, becomes a hanging closet on two levels for shirts and trousers in Craig Port's Cape Town warehouse. He hangs the rest of his wardrobe on an open rail in a niche.

because he needs moveable storage. Only real nomads can handle that kind of pruning of possessions.

To take stock of your storage needs within the available space, draw up a floor plan of your home that shows every storage opportunity, from closets to cabinets to plan chests. Then make a list of all the things that need to be put away, including the things that end up in piles in the kitchen. Even a wall hook for a wash bag or a laundry basket on top of the washing machine can make a difference. Each area has its own storage requirements, from the permanent to the portable.

In a converted industrial building, kitchens can be islands in the centre of the space or they can line up along a shared wall. A centralized kitchen needs clever storage figured out early on. Kitchen units that stand against a wall leave the floor space in front free for workstations on wheels, like butchers' blocks that offer workspace on top and drawers underneath. Avoid wall-mounted cupboards above worktops as they reduce the volume of space. Industrial dishwashers and refrigerators are also effective storage spaces. Rather than stacking your dishes onto ready-made shelving that is too narrow, measure your plates and build or find shelves that fit the dimensions. And remember that too much shelving is not

1 The locker room of a converted boarding school provides a wall of cupboards, a feature that the owners, Ronald Merens and Betty Bergen, have emphasized with a tall, narrow door and a ladder-like grid of light.

2 Architect Nico Rensch has exquisitely detailed storage with stacking, sliding boxes for clothes in his shower room.

3 In a loft conversion in London's Clerkenwell, architect Martin Lee has banked the wall behind his washbasin with yellow-painted panelling. A spring mechanism allows the panels to be lifted up, revealing niches for storage.

take on the proportions, but since they are not built-in they can move out with the owners.

Storage that moves suits a more nomadic lifestyle. Gym lockers offer freestanding storage that is less dated and more substantial than a clothes cupboard; coat-stands feature a rail for a pair of trousers, folding ladders with shelves, a tie rack, a mirror on top and shoe rail below. Chests of drawers are replaced by neatly stacked brown-paper-lined boxes and tin trunks. Tyler Brûlé, editor of the style magazine *Wallpaper*, keeps his wardrobe in five duffel bags that stand next to the airbed in his London apartment

3

1 Fine white grouting on the brick walls draws attention to a door that doubles as bookshelves in video producer Zanna's converted Battersea schoolhouse.

2 In another school conversion, the large, barn-like space allowed the owners to instal conventional bookshelves to house their library.

3 A wall of cupboards for china and serving dishes is saved from being too complicated by mesh panelling on each door that allows a glimpse of the interesting contents behind it.

always a good thing. Food storage is one of the areas where lifestyle will dictate your requirements. The professional living alone in a loft space with a freezer and a microwave, or the sushi take-away enthusiasts who are party animals, will not need shelving space for dried pasta and cans of tomatoes.

In the main living space, shelves and glass-doored cabinets, consoles and corner tables have been banished in favour of trolleys that house everything from the home-entertainment centre to the computer. Bookshelf units or a free-form partition wall fitted with shelves can divide a room and

hold any number of books and magazines, as well as art objects. Recycled wood barrels, stainless-steel tubs, wicker baskets and large terracotta jars all make characterful containers for umbrellas, throws, plants or extra pillows. Table tops are the new storage spaces, filling up with piles of magazines and papers stacked in colourful desk tidies and stationery boxes.

Sue Skeen took a utilitarian approach to storage. She had two rooms – a bedroom and bathroom – leading off a large, open-plan living, dining and cooking area. She designed her storage units, modelled in 1930s functional style, in pale wood, and stood them next to her chef's cooking range. Then she put castors on the rest of the

◀ *Clockwise from top left*: Clever converters on a small budget like to find new ways of using salvaged furniture. A shopkeeper's vitrine becomes a chest of drawers; a medical cabinet and a 1920s doctor's lamp make interesting additions to a dining room; bins that once held powder colours in a paint factory can hide a wealth of clutter; container crates on wheels make useful storage trolleys.

❶ In this Melbourne apartment, architect Bob Nation has created a thoroughly modern take on the built-in wardrobe.

❷ Designer Christopher Wood uses metal lockers for storage in this sleek bathroom.

furniture – styled like architectural plan chests and warehouse pallets for storage purposes – so that it could be moved about the maple floorboards. Storage items made from pale wood, chalky-white linen slipcovers on chairs, and aluminium detailing reflect watery light from the River Thames outside. Sue Skeen's taste is similar to her approach to life – style-conscious, but not too assertive, so there are no brand labels or designer images, just an edited collection with everything in its place and a place for everything.

Design Directory

UK Information

Advice

Architectural Association
34 Bedford Square
London WC1B 3ES

Association of Building
 Engineers
Jubilee House
Billingbrook Road
Northampton NN3 8NW

British Woodworking
 Federation
82 New Cavendish Street
London W1M 8AD
(Part of the Building Employers
Confederation. Publishes a list
of architects and contacts for
general joinery.)

The Building Centre
26 Store Street
London WC1E 7BT
(Information on everything to
do with building and building
materials. Offers advice to
members of the public on
general building enquiries.)

Chartered Society of Designers
32–38 Saffron Hill
London EC1N 8FH
(Contact the information section.)

The Cornflake Shop
37 Windmill Street
London W1P 1HH
(Sound systems and acoustic
advice.)

Council of Registered Gas
 Installers (CORGI)
1 Elmwood
Chineham Business Park
Crockford Lane
Basingstoke
Hants RG24 8WG
(All gas installation businesses
must register with CORGI.)

Crafts Council, Information Unit
44a Pentonville Road
London N1 9BY
(National organization for
promoting contemporary crafts.
For craftsmen and women,
apply for the Index of
Selected Makers.)

Design Council
1 Oxenden Street
London SW1Y 4EE

Electrical Contractors
 Association Ltd.
Esca House
34 Palace Court
London W2 4HY
(Publishes a list of members.)

Federation of Master Builders
Gordon Fisher House
14–15 Great James Street
London WC1N 3DP
(Contact regional office for
list of members: admits only
experienced builders.)

Heating and Ventilating
 Contractor's Association
Esca House
34 Palace Court
London W2 4JG

Institute of Plumbing
64 Station Lane
Hornchurch
Essex RM12 6NB
(Publishes regional lists of
members.)

Manhattan Loft Corporation
12 Queen Anne Street
London W1M 0AU

National Federation of Painting
 and Decorating Contractors
18 Mansfield Street
London W1M 9FG
(Publishes a list of members.)

National Federation of Roofing
 Contractors
24 Weymouth Street
London W1N 4LX
(Publishes a list of members.)

Royal Institute of British
 Architects
66 Portland Place
London W1N 4AD
(Ask for clients' advisory
service.)

Royal Institution of Chartered
 Surveyors
12 Great George Street
London SW1P 3AD

TRADA (Timber Research and
 Development Association)
Technology
Stocking Lane
Hughenden Valley
High Wycombe
Bucks HP14 4ND

Architectural Salvage

Architectural Heritage
Taddington Manor
Taddington
Cheltenham
Gloucestershire GL54 5RY

Architectural Salvage Centre
30–32 Stamford Road
London N1 4JL

Fens
46 Lots Road
London SW10 0QF

The House Hospital
68 Battersea High Street
London SW11 3HX

House of Steel
400 Caledonian Road
London N1 1DN

LASSCO
St. Michael &
 All Angels Church
Mark Street
London EC2A 4ER

Walcot Reclamation
108 Walcot Street
Bath BA1 5BG

Architects and Designers

Agenda Design Associates
IMA House
20 Northfields
London SW18 1PE

Allies and Morrison
42 Newman Street
London W1P 3PA

Architype Design Co-operative
4–6 The Hop Exchange
24 Southwark Street
London SE1 1TY

Arthur Collin Architects
1A Berry Place
London EC1V 0JD

Brian Ma Siy
Unit 2, 101 Amies Street
London SW11 2JW

Charles Rutherfoord
51 The Chase
London SW4 0NP

Circus Architects
1 Summers Street
London EC1R 5BD

Claudio Silvestrin
392 St. John's Street
London EC1Z 4NN

Cowper Griffiths Associates
15 High Street
Whittlesford
Cambridge CB2 4LT

CZWG
17 Bowling Green Lane
London EC1R 0BD

Domenico Rensch
Cheynes Farm
Warren Lane
Cotteridge
Herts SG9 9QA

Forge Architects & Surveyors
8–10 Lant Street
London SE1 1QR

Future Systems
199–205 Old Marylebone Road
London NW1 5QP

James Lambert Architects
5 St. John Street
London EC1M 4AA

Jenny Armit Interiors
167 Westbourne Grove
London W11 2RS

John Pawson
Unit B, 70–78 York Way
London N1 9AC

John Stefanidis
261 Fulham Road
London SW3

Jonathan McDowell
 & Renato Benedetti
62 Rosebery Avenue
London EC1R 4RR

Jonathan Woolf Architects
39–51 Highgate Road
London NW5 1RT

Lovegrove Studio
21 Powis Mews
London W11 1JN

Mark Guard Associates
161 Whitfield Street
London W1P 5RY

Martin Lee Associates
19 Rosebery Avenue
London EC1R 4SP

Munkenbeck and Marshall
3–11 Pine Street
London EC1R 0JH

Paxton Locher Architects
8 Clerkenwell Green
London EC1R 0DE

Powell-Tuck Associates
14 Barley Mow Passage
London W4 4PH

Richard Rogers Partnership
Thames Wharf
Rainville Road
London W6 9HA

Rick Mather Architects
123 Camden High Street
London NW1 7JR

Sergison Bates
44 Newman Street
London W1P 3PA

Tony Fretton
49–59 Old Street
London EC1V 9XH

Urban Splash
Concert Square Building
27 Fleet Street
Liverpool L1 6AR

Victoria Waymouth Interiors
30 Old Church Street
London SW3 5BY

Flooring

Afia Carpets
Chelsea Harbour
 Design Centre
Lots Road
London SW10 0XE

Altro Floors
Works Road
Letchworth
Herts SG6 1NW
(Rubber flooring.)

Amtico
The Amtico Co. Ltd.
Kingfield Road
Coventry CV6 5PL
(Vinyl flooring.)

Carpet Tile Centre
227 Woodhouse Road
London N12 9BD

English Woodlands Timber
Cocking Sawmills
Midhurst
West Sussex GU29 0HS

Forbo-Nairn Ltd.
PO Box 1
Kirkcaldy
Fife KY1 2SB
(Linoleum and vinyl floors.)

The Hardwood
 Flooring Company
146/152 West End Lane
London NW6 1SD
(New and reclaimed hardwood
floors and worktops.)

Interface Europe
Shelf Mills
Halifax
West Yorkshire HX3 7PA
(Tiles: tufted, fusion bonded,
fibre bonded.)

Kährs UK
Timberlaine Estate
Quarry Lane
Chichester
West Sussex PO19 2FJ
(Specialists in pre-finished
laminated flooring.)

Milland Fine Timbers Ltd.
Iping Road
Milland
Nr. Liphook
Hampshire GU30 0NA
(Suppliers of environmentally
managed hardwoods.)

Sinclair Till
793 Wandsworth Road
London SW8 3JQ

The West Sussex Antique
 Timber Company
Reliance Works
Newpound
Wisborough Green
West Sussex RH14 0AZ
(Salvage specialists also
offering new floors with an
'antiqued' finish.)

Wicanders
Amorium House
Star Road
Partridge Green
Horsham
West Sussex RH13 8RA
(Natural wood and cork floors.)

Lighting

Chelsea Lighting Design
Unit 1
23A Smith Street
London SW3 4EJ

Christopher Wray's
 Lighting Emporium
591 King's Road
London SW6 2YW
(Traditional and reproduction
designs.)

Concord Lighting
174 High Holborn
London WC1V 7AA
(Lighting system manufacturer.)

Erco Lighting
38 Dover Street
London W1X 3RB
(Hi-tech lighting systems
manufacturer.)

Fergus Cochrane
570 King's Road
London SW6 2DY
(Chandeliers.)

Forbes and Lomax Ltd.
205b St John's Hill
London SW11 1TH
('Invisible' transparent switches
and other types of switches.)

Imagination Ltd.
25 Store Street
London WC1 7BL
(Mostly commercial lighting
design.)

Isometrix Lighting & Design
8 Glasshouse Yard
London EC1A 4JN
(Mostly commercial work, but
some large-scale domestic
installations.)

John Cullen Lighting
585 King's Road
London SW6 2EH
(Low-voltage lighting
specialist.)

Lighting Design Partnership
3 John's Place
Edinburgh EH6 7EL

London Lighting Company
135 Fulham Road
London SW3 6RT

Mr Light
279 King's Road
London SW3 5EW

Whitecroft Lighting Ltd.
Burlington Street
Ashton-under-Lyne
Lancs OL7 0AX

Bathrooms

Aqualisa Products Ltd.
The Flyers Way
Westerham
Kent TN16 1DE

Armitage Shanks Ltd.
Armitage
Nr. Rugely WS15 4BT

Aston Matthews
141–147a Essex Road
London N1 2SN

Caradon Mira Ltd.
Cromwell Road
Cheltenham
Gloucestershire
GS52 5EP

C.P. Hart
Newnham Terrace
Hercules Road
London SE1 7DR

Czech & Speake
125 Fulham Road
London SW3 6RT

Dorset Reclamation
Cow Drove
Bere Regis
Wareham BH20 7JZ

Hansgrohe
Unit D1 & D2, Sandown Park
 Trading Estate
Royal Mills
Esher
Surrey KT10 8BL

Hydraspa
Unit D2, Crossgate Drive
Queen's Drive Industrial Estate
Nottingham
NG2 1LW

Ideal-Standard Ltd.
The Bathroom Works
Hull HU5 4HS

Jacuzzi UK
17 Mount Street
London W1Y 5RA

Max Pike Bathrooms
4 Ecclestone Street
London SW1W 9LN

Kitchens

Aga-Rayburn
PO Box 30
Ketley
Telford TF1 4DD

Appliance Care Ltd.
Grand Union House
Old Wolverton Road
Milton Keynes MK12 5ZR

ATAG UK Ltd.
19–20 Hither Green
Clevedon
Somerset BS21 6XU

Bulthaup UK Ltd.
37 Wigmore Street
London W1H 9LD

Buyers and Sellers
120 Ladbroke Grove
London W10 5NE

Kitchen Specialists' Association
PO Box 311
Worcester
Worcestershire WR1 1DN
(Members have at least two
years' experience.)

Miele Co. Ltd.
Fairacres
Marcham Road
Abingdon
Oxon OX14 1TW

Möben
Brindley Road
Old Trafford
Manchester M16 9HQ

Poggenpöhl
Filbury Court
368 Filbury Boulevard
Central Milton Keynes
MK9 2AF

SleMatic Möbelwerke
 GmbH & Co.
Osprey House
Rookery Court
Primett Road
Stevenage
Herts SG1 3EE

Whirlpool UK
PO Box 45
209 Purley Way
Croydon CR9 4RY

Furniture and Accessories

Aero
96 Westbourne Grove
London W2 5RT

Christopher Farr
 Handmade Rugs
115 Regents Park Road
London NW1 8UR

The Conran Shop
Michelin House
81 Fulham Road
London SW3 6RD
and
55 Marylebone High Street
London W1M 3AE

Harrods
Knightsbridge
London SW1

Harvey Nichols
Knightsbridge
London SW1

Heal's
196 Tottenham Court Road
London W1P 9LD

The Holding Company
241–245 King's Road
London SW3 5EL

IKEA
For the nearest branch contact:
Head Office
IKEA Brent Park
2 Drury Way
North Circular Road
London NW10 0TH

Jasper Morrison
92 Newark Street
London E1 2ES

Muji
26 Great Marlborough Street
London W1V 1HL

Purves & Purves
80–81, 83 Tottenham Court Rd
London W1P 9HD

Richard Taylor Designs
91 Princedale Road
London W11 4NS

Ron Arad
62 Chalk Farm Road
London NW1 8AN

SCP
135 Curtain Road
London EC2

Suzanne Ruggles
PO Box 201
London SW7 3DL
Tel: 0181 542 8476
  for appointment
(*Bold, elegant furniture in
hand-forged metal. Neo-
classical, Empire and Baronial
collections.*)

Viaduct
1–10 Summers Street
London EC1R 5BD

US Information

Advice

American Institute of Architects
1735 New York Avenue, NW
Washington
DC 20006

American Society of Interior
  Designers (ASID)
608 Massachusetts Avenue, NE
Washington
DC20002

American Society
  of Landscape Architects
4401 Connecticut Avenue, NW
Fifth Floor
Washington
DC 20008

Gas Appliance Manufacturer's
  Association (GAMA)
1901 North Moore Street
Suite 1100
Arlington
VA 22209
(*Publishes consumer directory
of certified efficiency ratings for
residential heating and water-
heating systems.*)

Hardwood Manufacturers
  Association
400 Penn Center Bld
Suite 530
Pittsburgh
PA 15235
(*Information on choosing and
maintaining hardwood floors.*)

The Hydronics Institute
35 Russo Place
PO Box 218
Berkeley Heights
NJ 07922
(*Provides pamphlets on hot-
water heating, radiant heating
and related topics.*)

National Association of
  Plumbing, Heating and
  Cooling Contractors
PO Box 6808
Falls Church
VA 22040
(*Answers inquiries about
plumbing, heating and cooling.*)

National Kitchen
  and Bath Association
687 Willow Grove Street
Hackettstown
NJ 07840-9988
(*Publishes an annual directory
of certified kitchen and bath
designers.*)

US Consumer Product Safety
  Commission
Washington
DC 20207
(*Publishes fact sheets on home
appliances.*)

Architects and Designers

Anderson/Schwartz Architects
180 Varick
New York
NY 10014

Annabelle Selldorf
Selldorf Architects
62 White Street
New York
NY 10013

Brian Murphy
1422 Second Street
Santa Monica
CA 90401

Gwathmey Siegel
475 10th Avenue
New York
NY 10018

John Beckmann
Axis Mundi
124 Watts Street
New York
NY 10013

Kiss & Zwigard
3rd Floor
60 Warren Street
New York
NY 10007

Peter Marino Architecture
150 East 58th Street
New York
NY 10022

Richard Lavenstein
(Bond Street)
Architecture & Design
33 Bond Street
New York
NY 10012

Tim Du Val Enterprises, Inc.
42–25 Vernon Boulevard
Long Island City
NY 11101

Lighting

Ballard Designs
1670 DeFoor Avenue
Atlanta
GA 30318

Broan Manufacturing Corp.
PO Box 140
Hartford
WI 53027

Digecon Plastics International
9160 Roe Street
Pensacola
FL 32514

Intermatic
777 Winn Road
Spring Grove
IL 60081

Lightolier
100 Lighting Way
Secaucus
NJ 07096

Luminaire
301 West Superior
Chicago
IL 60610

Thomas Industries
PO Box 769
1700 Gilbert Street
Hopkinsville
KY 42241

Flooring

American Hardwood Company
Distribution & Sales
15601 New Century Drive
Gardena
CA 90243

Ann Sacks Tile & Stone
115 Steward Street
Seattle
WA 98101

Armstrong World Industries
PO Box 441
Beaver Falls
PA 15010

Bruce Hardwood Floors
16803 Dallas Parkway
Dallas
TX 75248

Country Floors
15 East 16th Street
New York
NY 10003
and
8735 Melrose Avenue
Los Angeles
CA 90069

Dal Tile
7834 CF Hawn Freeway
Dallas
TX 75217

Empire Builders Supply
PO Box 5134
Santa Fe
NM 87502

Forbo Industries, Inc.
Humboldt Industrial Park
Maplewood Drive
PO Box 667
Hazleton
PA 18201

Johnsonite
A division of Duramex, Inc.
16910 Munn Road
Chagrin Falls
OH 44023

Kentucky Wood Floors
PO Box 33276
Louisville
KY 40232

Sheoga Hardwood Flooring and
Paneling, Inc.
PO Box 510
Burton
OH 44201

Tiles of Santa Fe, Inc.
PO Box 3767
Santa Fe
NM 87501

Index

Acknowledgments

Author's acknowledgments

The author would like to thank: Paula Hardy for her useful design directory; Jackie Ryan for her patience; Jess Walton for her memory bank; The Cornflake Shop for technical information on how to get the acoustics right in open spaces; Piers Gough at CZWG for practical information that makes conversions simpler, and for putting the fun back into functionalism; and all the owners, architects and designers of the beautiful homes carved out of the converted spaces featured in the gatefolds, for sharing with us all the problems and solutions encountered along the way.

Publisher's note

We would like to thank the further editors and designers who have contributed to this project: Gatefold copyediting: Christa Weil Proofreading: Tracey Beresford and Mandie Haynes Indexing: Peter Barber Typesetting: Peter Howard

We would also particularly like to thank the following people for allowing us to photograph and feature their homes in the gatefold pages of the book:
Andrée Putman
Fi McGhee
Kathleen van Zandweghe and Joris Mampaey
Barry Sack
Tim Du Val
Yuri Kuper and Morvane Achart

The publisher has made every effort to confirm the factual details contained in this book.

Picture research credits

1 Catherine Tighe Bogert (Architect: Andrew Berman); 2–3 Paul Rocheleau (Wynkoop DuBois Barn, Martha's Vineyard, MA); 8 Paul Rocheleau (Roher Barn, Lancaster, PA); 9 Anthony Staile/Archive Photos; 10 Verne Fotografie (Stuart Parr); 11 Richard Glover (Pattern House, London – Architect: Arthur Collin Architects); 12 Chris Gascoigne/View (Architects: CZWG); 13 left Gilles de Chabaneix/Daniel Rozensztroch/Marie Claire Maison (Designer: Murray Moss); 13 right Gilles de Chabaneix/Daniel Rozensztroch/Marie Claire Maison (Designer: Murray Moss); 14 15 Tumuli Township Schoolhouse, Winter 1993 Maxwell Mackenzie; 16 Earl Carter/Belle/Arcaid (Sophie Conran and Alex Willcock); 17 Christopher Wesnofske (Mr & Mrs Wesnofske, Bridgehampton, NY); 18 Reiner Blunck (Architect: Martin Leddy); 19 above Manuela Cerri (Architect: Edgar Vallora and Fausto Ghemi; Engineer: Giorgio Siniscalco); 19 centre left Michael Moran (Arthur Baker Loft, Jersey City – Architects: Abelow Connors Sherman Architects); 19 centre middle Jessie Walker (Architect: H Gary Frank AIA, Winnetka, Illinois); 19 centre right Reiner Blunck (Architect: Glenn Murcutt); 19 below left Monty Coles/Vogue Entertaining (Poppy King); 19 below centre Antoine Bootz (Laurence and William Kriegel – Architects: Edward Asfour and Peter Guzy); 19 below right Antoine Bootz (Laurence and William Kriegel – Architects: Edward Asfour and Peter Guzy); 20–21 Peter Aaron/Esto (Architects: Hanrahan Meyers, NY); 20 left Ted Yarwood (George Whiteside); 22 Pieter Estersohn/Lachapelle Representation (Designers: David McDermott and Peter McGough); 23 above Deidi von Schaewen (Daniel Vial, Provence); 23 below Antoine Rozes (Designer: Eugenie Collet); 24 left Michael Mundy/(Barbara de Vries and Alastair Gordon; 24–25 Todd Eberle (Rico Espinet and Heloisa Zero); 26 Catherine Tighe Bogert (Industria Superstudio, NYC – Architect: Andrew Berman); 27 Industria Superstudio, Milan; 28 Catherine Bibollet/Agence Top; 29 Henry Moore Sculpture Trust, Dean Clough, Halifax; 30 © 1993 Todd Eberle; 31 Marcus Leith/The Bankside Power Station; 32 Glasgow Museums and Art Galleries; 32 below Kevin Low (Tramway); 33 Kevin Low (Tramway); 34–35 Yigal Gawze; 36–37 Horst Neumann/JB Visual Press (The Kappeli Restaurant – Architects: Helka Perkkinen, Jukka Halminen and Aino Brandt); 37 right Alexander van Berge (Architect: Jaap Dijkman); 38 Yigal Gawze; 39 Deidi von Schaewen (Architect: Andrée Putman/ECART); 40–47 Deidi von Schaewen (Andrée Putman); 48 Chris Gascoigne/View (Architects: CZWG); 49 Roger Ressmeyer/Corbis; 50–51 Richard Glover (Pattern House, London – Architect: Arthur Collin Architects), 51 right John Edward Linden/Arcaid (Architect: Mark Guard); 52 Verne Fotografie (Architect: Ricardo Bofil); 53 left Eduard Hueber (Architects: Dean/Wolf Architects); 53 right Verne Fotografie (Architects: Kathleen van Zandweghe and Joris Mampaey); 54 above Deidi von Schaewen (Architect: Gilles Bouchez); 54 below Peter Aaron/Esto (Architects: Peter Forbes & Associates); 55 above Elliott Kaufman (Architects: Haigh Architects, Pual Haigh AIA & Barbara H. Haigh); 55 below Luc Wauman (Luc Verstraete and Isabelle Vermast – Architects: Peter Haverhals and Frank Heylen); 56 left John Edward Linden/Arcaid (Architect: Mark Guard); 56–57 Ray Main (Nick Allan); 58 Tim Goffe (Architects: Paxton Locher); 59 above left Deidi von Schaewen (Daniel Vial, Provence); 59 above right Mads Mogensen (Architects: Virginia Kerridge and Philip Wallace); 59 below left M. Grazia Branco/IKE-TRADE International (Designer: Ross Lovegrove); 59 below right Tim Beddow/The Interior Archive (Artist: Beazy Bailey, South Africa); 60–61 Gilles de Chabaneix/Marie Claire Maison; 61 above right Verne Fotografie (Architect: Ricardo Bofil); 61 below right Gilles de Chabaneix/Daniel Rozensztroch/Marie Claire Maison (Designer: Vicente Wolf); 62–68 Fi McGhee (Architect: John Pawson); 70 left Peter Aaron/Esto (Spaulding Taylor, San Francisco, California); 70 above right Patrick Leitner (Architect: Andrew Berman); 70 below right Ray Main (Architects: Circus Architects); 71 above Richard Glover (Vaight Apartment, London – Architects: Circus Architects); 71 below Tim Hawkins/Agenda Design Associates; 72 above Chris Gascoigne/View (Architects: Wells/Mackreth); 72 above centre Ray Main (Architects: Martin Lee Associates); 72 below left Peter Aprahamian (Architect: Nico Rensch); 72 right Eric Thorburn (Andre Tammes/Lighting Design Partnership); 73 Peter Aaron/Esto (Architects: Hanrahan Meyers, NY); 74 above Chris Gascoigne/View (Architects. Nick Hockley at ORMS); 74 below Deidi von Schaewen (Architect: Gilles Bouchez); 75 Elliott Kaufman (Haigh Architects, Paul Haigh AIA & Barbara H. Haigh); 76 above Deidi von Schaewen (Craig Port); 76 below Peter Aprahamian (Architect: Nico Rensch); 77 above Peter Aaron/Esto (Architects: Hanrahan Meyers, NY); 77 below Eric Thorburn/Glasgow Picture Library (Bob Callender and Liz Ogilvie); 78 Todd Eberle (Robert Indiana); 79 above Todd Eberle (Rico Espinet and Heloisa Zero); 79 centre Chris Meads ; 79 below Ted Yarwood (Curtis Wehrfritz – Architects: John Tong and Arriz Assam, 3rd UNCLE design Inc., Toronto); 80 Todd Eberle (LOT/EK Architecture – Ada Tolla and Giuseppe Lignano); 81 above left Julie Phipps/Arcaid (Architects: Cowper Griffith Associates); 81 above centre Richard Glover (Pattern House, London – Architect: Arthur Collin Architects); 81 above right Ray Main (Architects: St. John/Caruso Architects); 81 below left NicolasTosi/Catherine Ardouin/Marie Claire Maison (Architect: Narda rant Veer); 81 below centre Michael Moran (Arthur Baker Loft, Jersey City – Architects: Abelow Connors Sherman Architects); 81 below right Eduard Hueber (Architects: Dean/Wolf Architects); 82 Chris Gascoigne/View (Architects: CZWG); 83 Ted Yarwood (Designer: Richard Ferbrache); 84 above Antoine Rozes (Designer: Eugenie Collet); 84 below Gilles de Chabaneix/Catherine Ardouin/Marie Claire Maison (Thomas Wegner); 85 Andrew Bordwin (Architect: Paul Ochs); 86 above Chris Gascoigne/View (Architect: Suzanne Lumsden); 86 below Verne Fotografie (Architect: Vincent Van Duysen); 87 Wayne Vincent/The Interior Archive (Designer: Lee Mallet); 88–89 David Churchill/Arcaid (Patrick Hughes – Architects: Mark Willingale Associates); 89 right Michael Moran (Arthur Baker Loft, Jersey City – Architects: Abelow Connors Sherman Architects), 90 Peter Aaron/Esto (Ken Schroeder); 91 Otto Baitz/Esto (Architect: Kiss Cathcart Anders); 94 Ted Yarwood (Curtis Wehrfritz – Architects: John Tong and Arriz Assam, 3rd UNCLE design Inc., Toronto); 95 above left Manuela Cerri (Architect: Edgar Vallora and Fausto Ghemi; Engineer: Giorgio Siniscalco); 95 above right Gilles de Chabaneix/Catherine Ardouin/Marie Claire Maison (Thomas Wegner); 95 below left Manuela Cerri (Architect: Edgar Vallora and Fausto Ghemi; Engineer: Giorgio Siniscalco); 95 below right Christian Sarramon (DORIA, Paris); 96 above Richard Bryant/Arcaid (Architect: Gary Cunningham); 96 below Verne Fotografie (Stuart Parr); 97 Michael Moran (Arthur Baker Loft, Jersey City – Architects: Abelow Connors Sherman Architects); 98 Ray Main (Nick Allan); 99 Peter Aprahamian ©The Condé Nast PL/House and Garden 108 Chris Gascoigne/View (Architect: Suzanne Lumsden); 109 Paul Rocheleau (Private Barn, Sheffield, MA);

110 Gilles de Chabaneix/Daniel Rozensztroch/Marie Claire Maison (Designer: Murray Moss); 111 left Photographer: Jonathan Pile/Design: Project Orange; 111 right Catherine Tighe Bogert (Architect: Andrew Berman); 112–113 Richard Bryant/Arcaid (Architect: Gary Cunningham); 114 Wayne Vincent/The Interior Archive (Designer: Lee Mallet); 115 left Peter Aprahamian (Architect: Nico Rensch); 115 right Rodney Weidland/Vogue Living (Architect: Michael Rigg of Urban Spaces); 116 left Reiner Blunck (Architect: Glenn Murcutt); 116 right Jonathan Keenan Photography/Urban Splash (Shed Architects); 117 Eduard Hueber (Gruman & Sloan Loft – Architect: Anne Marie Baranowski); 118 above left Reiner Blunck (Architect: Martin Leddy); 118 below left Ray Main (Nick Allan); 118 below right Eric Thorburn (Andre Tammes/ Lighting Design Partnership); 118–119 above Ray Main (Architects: St. John/Caruso Architects); 120 above Peter Aaron/Esto (Architects: Peter Forbes & Associates); 120 below Todd Eberle (Robert Indiana); 121 Richard Bryant/Arcaid (Architect: Gwathmey Siegel & Associates); 122 Tim Soar (Oliver's Wharf – Architects: McDowell & Benedetti); 123–127 Tim Soar (Oliver's Wharf – Architects: McDowell & Benedetti); 130 Gilles de Chabaneix/Daniel Rozensztroch/ Marie Claire Maison (Alistair Gordon and Barbara De Vries); 131 above left M. Grazia Branco/ IKETRADE International (Designer: Ross Lovegrove); 131 above right Elliott Kaufman (Architects: Haigh Architects, Paul Haigh AIA & Barbara H. Haigh); 131 below right Richard Bryant/Arcaid (Architect: Gary Cunningham); 132 Peter Aaron/Esto (Architects: Peter Forbes & Associates); 133 above Marie Pierre Morel/Marie Kalt/Marie Claire Maison (Architect: Herve Vermesch); 133 below left Nicholas Kane/Arcaid (Architect: Ken Rorrison); 133 below right Verne Fotografie (Hilde Bouchez & Jan

Hoet); 134 above Gilles de Chabaneix/Catherine Ardouin/ Marie Claire Maison (Thomas Wegner); 134–135 below Peter Aaron/Esto (Architects: Hanrahan Meyers, NY); 135 above Eduard Hueber (Architect: Daniel O'Connor); 136 left Tim Hawkins/Agenda Design Associates; 136 right Alberto Piovano/Arcaid (Architect: Luigi Ferrario); 137 Eric Thorburn/ Glasgow Picture Library (Bob Callender and Liz Ogilvie); 138 Deidi von Schaewen (Craig Port); 139 Ted Yarwood (Curtis Wehrfritz – Architects: John Tong and Arriz Assam, 3rd UNCLE design Inc., Toronto); 142 Wulf Brackrock; 143 above Christian Sarramon (Windmill in Uitgeest, Holland); 143 below left Elliott Kaufman (Architects: Corinne Calesso/William Hallow – American Design Company); 143 below right Verne Fotografie (Hilde Bouchez & Jan Hoet); 144 left Peter Aaron/Esto (Architects: Hanrahan Meyers, NY); 144 right Peter Aaron/Esto (Architects: Hanrahan Meyers, NY); 145 Reiner Blunck (Architect: Martin Leddy); 148 Charlotte Wood (Architects: Cullum and Nightingale); 149 above left Ray Main (Architects: Martin Lee Associates); 149 above right Lu Jeffery (Alex Clive and Phoebe Woods-Humphrey); 149 below left Ted Yarwood (Curtis Wehrfritz – Architects: John Tong and Arriz Assam, 3rd UNCLE design Inc., Toronto); 149 below right Alberto Piovano/Arcaid (Architect: Luigi Ferrario); 150 left Jessie Walker (Architect: H Gary Frank AIA, Winnetka, Illinois); 150 right Elliott Kaufman (Architects: Ross Anderson at Anderson Architects); 151 Verne Fotografie (Architect: Coussee & Goris); 152 above Gilles de Chabaneix/Daniel Rozensztroch/ Marie Claire Maison (Laurence and William Kriegel – Architects: Edward Asfour and Peter Guzy); 152 below Max Jourdan (Zanna); 153 Teisseire Laurent/Catherine Ardouin/Marie Claire Maison (Tim & Carol Wood – Architects: Forge Architects); 154 above Verne Fotografie (Frank Destrooper); 154 below Peter

Aprahamian (Architect: Nico Rensch); 155 Richard Glover/ Arcaid (Architects: Circus Architects); 156 above Michael Mundy (Alistair Gordon and Barbara De Vries); 156 below Photographer Henry Bourne/ Producer: Mallery Lane/Elle Decoration (Owner/Designer: Jean Colonna); 157 above Ted Yarwood (George Whiteside); 157 below Eduard Hueber (Paula Iacucci); 158 Deidi von Schaewen (Artist: Arranz Bravo); 159 Luc Wauman (Luc Verstraete and Isabelle Vermast – Architects: Peter Haverhals and Frank Heylen); 160–161 Lizzie Himmel (Tim Du Val); 162 Antoine Bootz (Tim Du Val); 165 Lizzie Himmel (Tim Du Val); 166 above right and below left Antoine Bootz (Tim Du Val); 166 above left and below right Lizzie Himmel (Tim Du Val); 167 Lizzie Himmel (Tim Du Val); 168 above Luc Wauman (Joris Ghekiere and Inge Henneman – Architect: Hugo Kinnear); 168 below Rodney Weidland/Vogue Living (Architect: Ray Gill); 169 Reiner Blunck (Architect: Glenn Murcutt); 170 Luc Wauman (Ronald Merens and Betty Bergen); 171 above John Edward Linden/Arcaid (Architect: Mark Guard); 171 below R. Weidland/Vogue Living (Architect: Michael Rigg of Urban Spaces); 172 Julie Phipps/Arcaid (Architects: Cowper Griffith Associates); 173 Eduard Hueber (Gruman & Sloan Loft – Architect: Anne Marie Baranowski); 174 left Ted Yarwood (Designer: Christopher Wood – LA Design); 174–175 Eric Thorburn/Glasgow Picture Library (Bob Callender and Liz Ogilvie); 176 Tim Beddow/The Interior Archive (Artist: Beazy Bailey, South Africa); 177 Earl Carter/Vogue Living (Kaarin and Ken Wallace – Architects: Don McQuatter and Julie Meacham); 178 Pieter Estersohn/ Lachapelle Representation (Designers: David McDermott and Peter McGough); 179 above left Ted Yarwood (Jeff Roick); 179 above right Verne Fotografie (Stuart Parr); 179 centre left Jean-Francois Jaussaud

(Designer: Julie Prisca, Normandy); 179 centre right Verne Fotografie (Architects: Stamberg – Aferiat); 179 below left Luc Wauman (Ronald Merens and Betty Bergen); 179 below right Rodney Weidland/Vogue Living (John Pegrum and Dayne van Bree); 180–181 Antoine Bootz (Laurence and William Kriegel – Architects: Edward Asfour and Peter Guzy); 181 right Gross and Daley (Decorator: Gwynn Griffith, San Antonio, Texas); 182 left Wayne Vincent/The Interior Archive (Designer: Lee Mallet); 182 right Verne Fotografie (Piet Goossens); 183 Fritz von der Schulenburg/The Interior Archive; 184 Verne Fotografie (Architect: James Biber, Pentagram, NY); 185 Jean-Francois Jaussaud (Designer: Julie Prisca, Normandy); 186 above left M. Grazia Branco/IKETRADE International (Designer: Ross Lovegrove); 186 above right Eduard Hueber (Architects: Dean/Wolf Architects); 186 below left Ted Yarwood (Curtis Wehrfritz – Architects: John Tong and Arriz Assam, 3rd UNCLE design Inc., Toronto); 186 below right Reiner Blunck (Architect: Martin Leddy); 187 Dennis Gilbert/View (Architects: AHMM); 188–189 above Anthony Johnson/House & Leisure (Craig Port); 189 above right Max Jourdan (Zanna); 189 below Simon Upton/World of Interiors (Designer: Sue Skeen); 190 above M. Grazia Branco /IKE-TRADE International (Designer: Ross Lovegrove); 190 below left Alan Weintraub/Arcaid (Architect: Bryon Cuth and Elizabeth Ranyeri); 190 below right Richard Bryant/Arcaid (Architect: Gary Cunningham); 191 Peter Aaron/Esto (Spaulding Taylor, San Francisco, California); 192 Verne Fotografie (Designer: Vicente Wolf); 193 left Photographer: Jonathan Pile/Design: Project Orange; 193 right Gilles de Chabaneix/ Daniel Rozensztroch/Marie Claire Maison (Designer: Murray Moss); 194 left M. Grazia Branco/IKE-TRADE International (Designer: Ross Lovegrove); 194 right

Ted Yarwood (Curtis Wehrfritz – Architects: John Tong and Arriz Assam, 3rd UNCLE design Inc., Toronto); 195 Christophe Dugied/ World of Interiors (Artist and Glass Designer: Marie Ducate); 196 Verne Fotografie (Architect: Charles Cowles); 197 above left Dennis Gilbert/View (Architects: AHMM); 197 above centre Gilles de Chabaneix/Daniel Rozensztroch/Marie Claire Maison (Designer: Murray Moss); 197 above right M. Grazia Branco/IKE-TRADE International (Designer: Ross Lovegrove); 197 centre left and right Ray Main (Architects: Circus Architects); 197 centre middle Simon Wheeler/The Sunday Times/Times Newspapers Ltd. (Designer: Ross Lovegrove); 197 below left Verne Fotografie (Designer: Vicente Wolf); 197 below centre Christoph Kicherer (Architects: St. John/Caruso Architects); 197 below right Lu Jeffery (Alex Clive and Phoebe Woods-Humphrey); 198–205 Jean-Pierre Godeaut (Yuri Kuper); 206 left M. Grazia Branco/IKE-TRADE International (Designer: Ross Lovegrove); 206 – 207 Anthony Johnson/ House & Leisure (Craig Port); 208 left Luc Wauman (Ronald Merens and Betty Bergen); 208 right Peter Aprahamian (Architect: Nico Rensch); 209 Ray Main (Architects: Martin Lee Associates); 210 left Max Jourdan (Zanna); 210 right Nicolas Tosi/Catherine Ardouin/ Marie Claire Maison (Architect: Narda van t Veer); 211 Gilles de Chabaneix/Daniel Rozensztroch/ Marie Claire Maison (Laurence and William Kriegel – Architects: Edward Asfour and Peter Guzy); 212 above left Antoine Rozes (Designer: Eugenie Collet); 212 above right Jean-Francois Jaussaud (Lendon Flanagan, L.A.; Designers: David Cruz (Blackman & Cruz), L.A.); 212 below left Deidi von Schaewen (Craig Port); 212 below right Antoine Rozes (Designer: Eugenie Collet); 213 left Ted Yarwood (Designer: Christopher Wood – LA Design); 213 right Earl Carter/Belle/Arcaid (Architect: Bob Nation/Stylist: Zinta Jurjans-Heard).